THE RACIALIZATION OF SLAVERY

by

R.L. Worthy

KornerStone Books
6947 Coal Creek Pkwy
Suite 206
Newcastle, WA 98059
Ksbooks@execs.com

Published by

KornerStone Books
6947 Coal Creek Pkwy
Suite 206
Newcastle, WA 98059
Ksbooks@execs.com

Copyright ©2009 R. L. Worthy

All Rights Reserved. No part of this publication may be reproduced, stored in a retrieval system or transmitted in any form or by any means electronic, mechanical, photocopying, recording or otherwise, without the prior written permission of the publisher.

Design and Layout: KornerStone Books

Unless otherwise stated, all images courtesy of The Hall of Records - KornerStone Books ©

Printed in the United States of America

The First Edition

ISBN: 978-0-9727627-8-6

"The heart fails not he who remembers yesterday . . . As for the man without experience who listens not, he effects nothing what-so-ever. He sees knowledge in ignorance, profit in loss; he commits all kinds of error, always choosing the contrary of what is praiseworthy."

Prologue:

In the 19th century, the British intellectual Sir Godfrey Higgins would explain that he had been consigned to spend the entire latter part of his life *"unlearning the nonsense,"* he had been taught in his youth. I believe it apropos to begin this book with his observation insomuch as two centuries later I find myself having to do the same thing!

Unfortunately, many in the West believe that it is the responsibility of the old to lie to the young. *They even espouse the view that by merely lying to two consecutive generations, an artifice will become real in the minds of those they mislead.* Of course, the collapse of the corrupt regimes of the past renders this nothing more than a liar's fantasy: *". . . you can't fool all of the people all of the time."* Nevertheless, the need to convince everyone within the sound of their voice that they are infallible, and in control, has impaired their reason—*they've confused a willingness to misinform the unsuspecting with brilliance.*

Historically speaking, Socrates is recognized as inventing the artifice of lying to the masses to maintain control over them. His plan was to teach the Greek populace from a young age that it was God's will that they be utilized (*as in used up*) by the powerful. In these times the tune that's most often trumpeted is <u>a wealthy amoral few know what's best for the vast majority of us</u>. Consequently, about the only time the powerful want to engage the masses today is to bolster some old lie, or to advance a new one . . .

But I digress—getting back to Higgins, dismayed by the falsehoods disseminated throughout Europe in matters of history, religion and race—in 1833 he wrote, <u>Anacalypsis: An Attempt To Throw Aside The Vail Of The Sisaticisis Or An Inquiry Into The Origins Of Nations, Languages And Religions</u>. To his great credit, Higgins would forthrightly dispel many of the period's race-based fallacies. Not only would he acknowledge many of the achievements of the Black Race, he would also declare: *"I think it right to make an observation upon an effect of prejudice, which has operated for the concealment of truth in modern times more than any other cause what-so-ever . . ."*

Regrettably, two hundred years later, I must contend that little has changed in many parts of the West. Today, the truth is constantly censored when it comes to the historic exploits of the Black Race. Despite an obsession with trying to depict ancient Blacks as mindless tree dwellers—the truth is that they were not swinging on branches, but exceptionally well-grounded. *As a matter of fact, their feet were so firmly planted that they would not just master their immediate environs—but traverse this globe as well!*

Even those who are considered to have a *"good American education,"* know next to nothing about the magnificent contributions of the Black Race to human progress: for example, the earliest nation-states were created by Blacks; the world's first empirical scientists and doctors were Black; the world's first architects and construction engineers were Black; the first sailors of the high seas were Black; Greek culture and mythology were spawned in earlier Black civilization; Blacks would play a pivotal role in the history of the Roman Empire; and, the foundations of several of man's most prominent modern religions were laid by the Black Race! Truth be told, Blacks were at the forefront of man's greatest achievements for millenniums.

Yet, not only are such findings ignored by American educators—*race-based lies are often substituted and celebrated instead.*

A tragic consequence of this ploy is the idea that Blacks are intellectually inferior to Whites. Further, racial slavery has been an indispensable tool for those seeking to uphold this invention. The case is easily made that nothing has proven a bigger impediment to the overall growth of Blacks and Whites (*as individuals*) and America (*as a nation*) than the racialized view of slavery.

Look, around the world it is a well-known fact that people of all races have experienced slavery through the ages. Hence, any argument that "*Black is synonymous with slavery and/or ignorance*" is absolutely ridiculous: *hmmm'* . . . 5,000 years of recorded history—let's see, we will just tell em' about 3 or 4 centuries and disregard, or lambaste, the other 46 hundred!

This is a stratagem that immediately brings to mind the Orwellian pronouncement: *"The really frightening thing about totalitarianism is not that it commits 'atrocities' but that it attacks the concept of objective truth; it claims to control the past as well as the future."*

In light of the fact that the common perception is so far afield from the truth, I am compelled to pen, The Racialization of Slavery. Please take a moment to look at the images on the back cover: AF (blue) represents our basic anatomical functions; IR (green) represents information reception; and, PS (red) represents problem solving and future planning. Though rudimental, these diagrams impart the fact that once human perception fails to square with reality, we blunder. What's more, we will continue to make mistakes until our perceptions are corrected. Expressed in other terms, *garbage in—garbage out . . .*

Black parents, *you immerse your children in a biased educational system and culture—and are then astonished that they grow up confused, frustrated, and unfulfilled.* <u>*Those with no care for the past and future—have nowhere to go*</u> *. . .*

White parents, *while it seems like the fanciful pact you embrace is just grand for your posterity—the arc is long but it bends toward justice! "Familiarize yourself with the chains of bondage and you prepare your own limbs to wear them." Thus, the question is,* <u>*what are you consigning your posterity to*</u>*?*

Finally, ***Parents and teachers***, *you can ignore all of this if you wish, but school age children in ancient Egypt understood that "a lie can't live forever!" Upon reflection, little wonder that a century ago H.G. Wells should say: "*<u>*Human history becomes more and more a race between education and catastrophe*</u> *. . ."*

THUS, THIS EFFORT

CONTENTS

Timeless Wisdom — iii

Prologue — iv

Table of Contents — xii

Skin Color — 1

The Color Of The Curse — 28

The Enslavement Of Caucasians Through The Ages — 45

The Portuguese Enter Africa — 58

Spain & New World — 70

The Hues Of Slavery In North America — 78

The 16th Century Advent Of The Negro — 96

Black In The Old World — 114

CONTENTS

The Transatlantic Trafficking Of Human Beings   122

Cultural Ties & Distant Lineages   151

Treatment Of The Enslaved Through The Ages   162

African Freedom Fighters   175

Epilogue   212

Bibliography   214

Index   234

Past Reviews   242

Discount Order Form   243

Skin Color

THE RACIALIZATION OF SLAVERY

In that physical appearance has played such a large role in the "divide and control" stratagem—let me begin here with a word about human skin color. Activated melanin is the biological substance that produces skin color in Homo Sapien Sapiens (Human Beings). Basically speaking, the more activated melanin one has—the richer, or more color the person has—the less, the paler.[1] Peoples whose skin is black and brown possess more activated melanin than people whose skin is paler (*most often described as yellow, red, or white*). As anthropologists have established that the earliest Homo Sapien Sapiens had black (actively melaninized) skin, the question is—*How did today's populations with lower concentrations*

---

[1] Biological Coloration, The Encyclopedia Britannica Vol. XVI, p. 588 & Sek-kem, G., Melanin and the Next Millennium: The Kem-Wer Factor pp. 9 - 10

Activated melanin is a dominant—not recessive—trait in human beings. In other words, a population that is not able to produce activated melanin (or pale) cannot produce a population with high levels of activated melanin (or black).

of activated melanin come about? The answer lies in the cold glaciated mountains of Asia during the Achen Glacial Age.

The Geography

Briefly, geologists explain that 60,000 years ago Central Asia's climatic conditions were such that it was possible for actively melaninized (black and/or brown) populations to reach and settle in her mountainous passes. It is further explained that in the 10,000 years between the Wurm II and Achen glacial periods, some tribes began to migrate out of the equatorial belt into the higher elevations of Central and Northeastern Asia. However, with the coming of the Achen Glacial period, the climate changed so drastically that once easily traveled mountainous routes became sealed by glaciers and severe cold for millenniums!

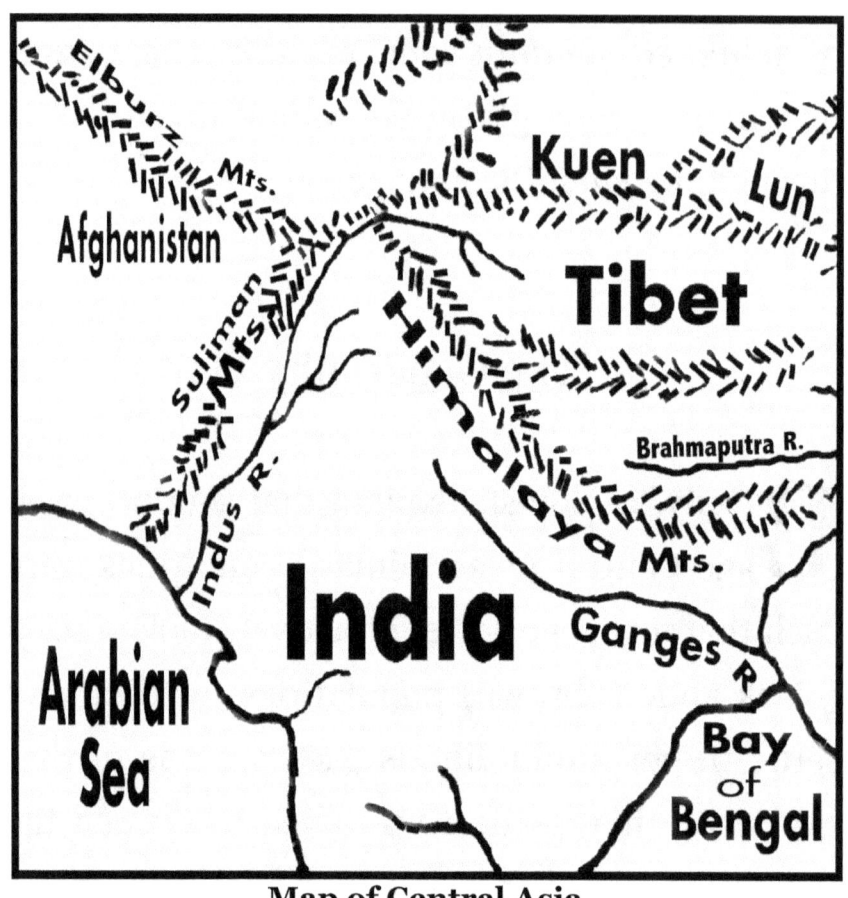
Map of Central Asia

According to Kephart:

> "*It was the minor Achen glaciation, whose effects began to seriously be felt about 25,000 years ago. It impelled the descent of the majority of the Aryan [brown] inhabitants of the Indus valley from their*

upper settlements southward to warmer climes; they were the later Indonesians (Polynesians). Those who had reached and settled in the valleys of the high Indus River and its tributaries, such as the Shyok, between the Himalayan and Karakoram mountain ranges in eastern Ladak and the lake region of the northwestern Tibetan provinces of Ngari and Rudok, were permanently separated from those who had retreated down the Indus. The passes over the Suliman Mountains to Afghanistan and Iran also were closed. These inhabitants who thus were isolated in the broad unglaciated river valleys and around the numerous warm-water lakes of eastern Ladak and western Tibet (the lake regions of central and northwestern Tibet are conspicuous for their great number of widely distributed hot springs, which tend to modify the extreme climate of the country during and after glaciations) during this glacial period are noteworthy as having been the progenitors of the white Keltic and Nordic branches of the Aryan [or Brown] race..."[2]

The empirical evidence (*as stated by respected anthropologists, historians, and biologists*) leaves no doubt that tens of millenniums ago the

---

[2] Kephart, C., Races of Mankind pp. 22, 30 - 32, 49 - 56, 66 - 67, 154, 230, 187, 278 - 279 & Hoebel, E., Anthropology: The Study of Man p. 103 & De Graft-Johnson, J., African Glory p. 6 & (Video), The Living Body: Skin Deep & Aoumiel, Dancing Shadows: The Roots of Western Religious Beliefs p. 4, 15
A point of clarification here: the ancient Aryans that Kephart is discussing were indeed actively melaninized. By way of illustration, he also explains: *"Some of the Ethiopians remained in Southern Iran until after the time of Herodotus. All of these southern (or Ethiopian) Aryans comprised what are known as the Hamitic [Black] people."* In addition, Aoumiel makes associations between the ancient Aryans and the ancient Hittites who were Canaanites (Hamites). While I make no apology for sharing Kephart's research (as someone trained in physical anthropology) his terminology, in this instance, leaves a bit to be desired—culturally speaking.

progenitors of the Nordic Caucasian were actively melaninized. In the words of the formerly noted:

> *"The light-complexioned peoples [developed] during and after the glaciation in the cold regions of the high Himalayas or the far North. The Keltic and Nordic and the Finnic peoples represent blond or near blond elements of the Aryan [Brown] and the Turanian [Yellow] races respectively that evolved in cold, bleak regions, the first two in the sheltered vales of Ladak and western Tibet during the Achen glaciation and the other on the highlands of eastern Tibet and along the headwaters of the Yenisei River in Siberia."*[3]

---

[3] Rogers, J.A., Sex and Race Vol. I, p. 63 & Higgins, G., Anacalypsis Vol. I, p. 434 & Kephart, C., Races of Mankind pp. 30 - 32, 52 - 53, 55 - 56, 66 - 67, 154, 230, 278 - 279 & Hoebel, E., Anthropology: The Study of Man p. 103 & De Graft-Johnson, J., African Glory p. 6 & (Video), The Living Body: Skin Deep & Burn, A., & Selincourt, A., Herodotus:

Aryan

Whereas so much racial confusion exists over the term <u>Aryan</u>, permit me to provide you with a few facts about the word and its use. The name Aryan is actually derived from a term that was created and utilized by Old World Blacks. This is clear, as the culture and territories of the ancient Medes (Madai) and Persians (Parsa) were originally Elamite. Indo-Europeans did not arrive in this part of the world until well after the term's creation.[4]

<u>The Histories</u> p. 466 & Collins, R., <u>Medes and Persians: Conquers & Diplomats</u> pp. 10 - 15 & Benedict, R., <u>Race: Science and Politics</u> pp. 14 - 15 & Montagu, A., <u>Man's Most Dangerous Myth: The Fallacy of Race</u> p. 31 & Benedict, R., & Weltfish, G., <u>The Races of Mankind</u> p. 11 & Synder, L., <u>Race: A History of Modern Ethnic Theories</u> pp. 86 - 89

[4] Aoumiel, <u>Dancing Shadows: The Roots of Western Religious Beliefs</u> p. 4, 15 & Rogers, J.A., <u>Sex and Race</u> Vol. I, p. 63, 151, 265 & Higgins, G., <u>Anacalypsis</u> Vol. I, p. 434 & Kephart, C., <u>Races of Mankind</u> pp. 30 - 32, 52 - 53, 55 - 56, 66 - 67, 154, 230, 278 - 279 & Hoebel, E., <u>Anthropology: The Study of Man</u> p. 103 & De Graft-Johnson, J., <u>African Glory</u> p. 6 & Burn, A., & Selincourt, A., <u>Herodotus: The</u>

THE SCIENCE OF SKIN COLOR

Map of Southwestern Asia

Histories p. 466 & Collins, R., Medes and Persians: Conquers & Diplomats pp. 10 - 15 & Koch, R., The Book of Signs p. 18 & Clegg, R., Mackey's Revised History of Freemasonry & Becker, U., The Continuum Encyclopedia of Symbols pp. 289 - 291 & Biedermann, H., Dictionary of Symbolism p. 334 & Quinn, M., The Swastika p. 1 & Fylfot, The Universal Standard Encyclopedia Vol. X, p. 3558 Let me also say a word about the symbol today known as the Swastika. This symbol is not a recent creation but quite ancient. It originally it had nothing to do with hate—but munificence! Also known as the Fylfot, the symbol's earliest use dates back to the 5th millennium BCE and the Black peoples of Asia (see footnote pages 25 - 27).

The Racialization of Slavery

For brevity's sake, allow me to share the following analysis of this matter by Ashley Montagu:

> *"The term 'Aryan' is frequently misused to describe a physical stock or alleged member of that stock. In reality it refers to a stock of languages which are spoken by a wide variety of ethnic groups. It has nothing whatever to do with physical characters."*

Likewise, in their <u>The Races of Mankind</u>, Benedict and Weltfish write: *"As Hitler uses it, the term "Aryan" has no meaning, racial, linguistic, or otherwise . . ."* Yet, forasmuch as no author has delineated the issue more succinctly, I will end here with this comment by Snyder: *"The attempt of Aryan racialists in contemporary Germany to attribute ideal racial qualities to both early Indo-Europeans and present-day Nordics may be dismissed as a political rationalization having no scientific support...*"⁵

Ancient Elamite in Palace of Darius I c. 500 BCE

---

⁵ Benedict, R., Race: Science and Politics pp. 14 - 15 & Montagu, A., Man's Most Dangerous Myth: The Fallacy of Race p. 31 & Benedict, R., & Weltfish, G., The Races of Mankind p. 11 & Synder, L., Race: A History of Modern Ethnic Theories pp. 86 - 89

In 484 CE, the famous chronicler Moses of Khorene would characterize Western Asia thus: *"The name of Kush or Ethiopia applies to four great regions, Media, Persia, Susiana or Elam, and Aria [Northern Arabia] or to the whole territory between the Tigris and Indus [Southeastern Pakistan]."*

THE RACIALIZATION OF SLAVERY

Mountainous glacier in Southern Asia

Deactivated Melanin

Hence, spending several millenniums in isolated and inclement environs accounts for the Caucasian Race's lower sweat gland distribution, non-activated melanin, propensity for fat retention, and condensed limb and muscle structure. The reasons for these biological adaptations are as follows: (1), the lower distribution of sweat glands helped to conserve heat; (2), the accumulation of white adipose cells (fat) served to store energy; (3), the brown adipose (fat) cells served to generate heat; and (4), fat tissue on the limbs served to insulate and ward off frostbite. By contrast, elongated limbs and lean muscle (though denser) promote heat diffusion throughout the body.

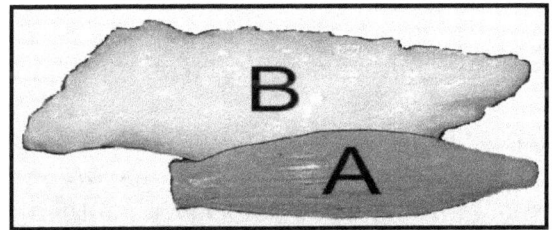

Scale illustration of 5 lbs of muscle (A) and 5 lbs of fat (B)

THE RACIALIZATION OF SLAVERY

What's more, the cold and sunless environment would prove detrimental to those with higher degrees of activated melanin. Gloger explains that the deficiency of vitamin D due to the lack of ultraviolet radiation (sunlight) in these regions made it more difficult for those with greater concentrations of activated melanin to survive. As the number of those with activated melanin became smaller and smaller, eventually, the melanin in this population lost its ability to activate: they all became pale. Rogers states:

> "Sergi of the University of Rome, denied that there was a European race. European man, he said was African man, changed by the effects of European environment."[6]

---

[6] Rogers, J.A., Sex and Race Vol. I, pp. 29 - 30 & Simon, L., Iberia and the Mediterranean World of the Middle Ages p. 389

Brinton wrote: "The most completely white communities are found among the Slavonic populations of Southern and Central Russia. Their hair is colorless and their complexion so near a 'dead white' . . . one anthropologist (Theodor

Ancient Caucasian in Asia c. 2500 BCE

Posche) has selected the vast Roketno swamps as the original home of the white race which he thinks arose by endemic albinism." Photo of Baltoro Glacier (page 12) appears courtesy of Guilhem Vellut and Wikimedia CC-BY-SA-2.0.

THE RACIALIZATION OF SLAVERY

So, in summary, the racial classification of Caucasian is made up of people whose melanin lost its properties of activation after being hemmed in the cold and sunless mountains of Asia for millenniums. Conversely, the branch of humanity possessing activated melanin today (the darker races) are in fact the descendants of the peoples who inhabited the sunny and warmer River Valleys of the Nile, Tigris, Euphrates, and Indus during the concurrent millenniums.

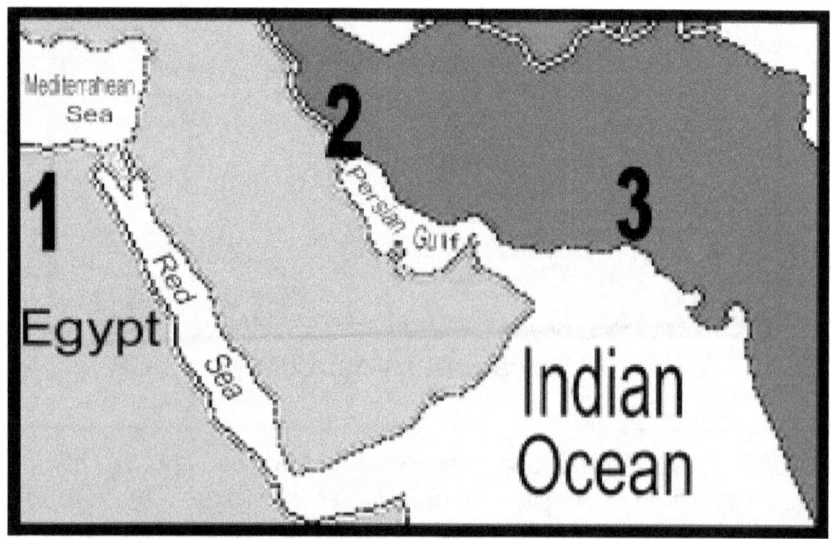

(1) Nile (2) Tigris & Euphrates (3) Indus - River Valleys

Activated Melanin

Having found that the skin color of the first humans was black (actively melaninized) and that pale (white) skin is caused by melanin that's lost its activation capability—allow me to share a few more findings about activated melanin:

> First, *what is melanin?* Scientists explain: *"Melanins are polymers (compounds consisting of repeating units) of variable mass and complexity. They are synthesized from the amino acid Tyrosine by progressive oxidation, a process catalyzed by the copper containing enzyme Tyrosinase . . ."* Researchers go on: *"There are two types of melanin: eumelanin (black melanin), and phaeomelanin (dun, or orange to red melanin) . . . A granule of either type of melanin starts out as a colorless ball inside a membranous container. If destined to*

become eumelanin, it turns into a flattish oval body with concentric laminations. As time goes on, it begins to become pigmented and its structure becomes blurred, unless it is a dud—scheduled to remain colorless. Fully ripened granules are flat, blackish discs between 1.3 and 1.0 microns long and between 0.6 and 0.5 microns wide."

Activated melanin is not, *nor ever has been*, a recessive biological trait in human beings. The Albino population happens to be the group with the least amount of activated melanin. Unfortunately, they regularly face a myriad of physiological illnesses that other populations do not.

Melanin absorbs the ultra-violet rays of the sun, which means actively melaninized skin is able to absorb more heat than skin without. As a matter of fact, researchers explain that many Blacks do not get sunburn. Moreover, activated melanin is believed to act as a block from the harmful rays of the sun, which gives the darker races greater protection from sun damage and/or skin cancers. Activated melanin is also considered to retard the aging process.

Organic chemist Carol Barnes maintains that during the day melanin provides the advantageous function of serving like seratonin (a derivative of the important amino acid Tryptophan), while acting as an alkaloid (or stimulus for the nervous system) at night.

Kinesiology Professor Malachi Andrews maintains that it is the neuromelanin in the brain stem and cerebellum that helps to facilitate complex and rhythmic motor function in humans.

In Racial Adaptations we read:
"*Pigmentation varies racially in two parts of the eye. One is the outer surface of the retina . . . Rays of visual light that pass through it enter two glands in the brain that speed up or slow down the reaction of our nervous systems to stimuli. The amount of light that reaches these glands depends partly on retinal color; as a result there are racial differences in certain aspects of behavior. Pink and yellow retinas reflect light that darker ones absorb; they slow reactions down, while darker retinas speed them up.*"
Individuals with lower concentrations of

melanin in their irises are also more likely to develop cataracts from long time exposure to ultraviolet radiation.

Activated melanin even facilitates the safe reception of many of the biological benefits of sunlight. For instance, scientists have noted the following benefits from exposure to time-cherished sunlight: (1), it can lower blood pressure; (2), it helps to synthesize vitamin D in the skin; (3), it brings the body into contact with ultraviolet rays which kill several types of harmful bacteria; (4), it stimulates the pineal gland (known as the Seat of the Soul) through the eye; (5), it may very well lower cholesterol levels in the blood; and (6), it is even explained that the platelets of our red and white blood cells function more efficiently when in sunlight than in darkness! In the words of Lillyquist:

> *"As it enters our eyes, sunlight triggers internal processes that affect blood, bones, protein level, and numerous glands and organs. Sunlight can increase our resistance to a number of diseases and even cure some. Without sunlight, we lose muscle tone and become weak, sexually apathetic, and depressed. Christoph*

Hufeland was probably the first to comment on the necessity of sunshine for normal human functioning when, in his 1797 book, **The Art of Prolonging Life**, *he observed the devitalized state of persons sequestered over long period in dungeons. Their poor appearance was due not, he thought, to poor diet and lack of recreation, but to the absence of the sun's beneficence."*

Modern scientists have spent years studying the properties of melanin in hopes of manufacturing a synthetic form of this polymer. Biologists have tried to manufacture synthetic melanin from the cuttle fish, squid, black caviar and even mushrooms. Of course, one of the most obvious reasons for this is that skin cancer (melanoma) in Caucasians, caused by the ultra-violet rays of sunlight, is not only occurring at an alarming rate—it is rising. Dr. Dean Myers warns that just one severe sunburn can greatly increase the risk of developing the cancer. A potentially deadly disease, metastatic melanoma can spread to the brain, lymph nodes, lungs, liver and bones.

Further, scientists explain that the continuing depletion of the Ozone Layer will cause people without activated melanin to become even more susceptible to this cancer. In actuality, scientists have already noted a doubling in the rate of melanoma in Australia. Remarkably, Gore explains: *"In Queensland, in northeastern Australia, for example, more than 75 percent of all its citizens who have reached the age of sixty-five now have some form of skin cancer, and children are now required by law to wear large hats and scarves to and from school to protect from ultraviolet radiation."* Additionally, the American Academy of Dermatology says, on average, one person dies from melanoma every hour—and the disease is increasing faster than any other form of cancer . . .

In conclusion, Wills makes the following disclosure about melanin and skin color: *"The master enzyme in all this is tyrosinase. If the gene for this enzyme is defective, the result is a person with albinism, someone who makes no melanin at all. But the most remarkable discovery made by molecular biologists has been that most of us, regardless of skin color, have quite enough tyrosinase in our melanocytes to make us very black. In those of us with light skin, something is preventing the enzyme from functioning at full capacity . . ."*[6]

---

[6] Wills, C., The Skin We're In Discover Nov. 15, No. 11 Nov. 1994 pp. 79 - 80 & Coon, C., Racial Adaptations pp. 48 - 51, 94 - 95, 97 & Sunderland, E., Elements of Human and Social Geography pp. 59 - 60 & Shapiro, H., Race Mixture p. 30 & Montagu, A., Man's Most Dangerous Myth: The Fallacy of Race p. 132 & Adipose, Encyclopedia of Human Biology Vol. I, pp. 61 - 62 & Montagu, A., The Concept of Race pp. 140 - 141 & Biological Coloration, The Encyclopedia Britannica Vol. XVI, p. 588 & Sek-kem, G., Melanin and the Next Millennium: The Kem-Wer Factor & Milele, N., The Journey of the Songhai People pp. 46 - 51 & Evolution, Human The Encyclopedia Britannica Vol. XVIII, p. 845 & Pierpaoli, W., Regelson, W., & Colman, C., The Melantonin Miracle pp. 70 - 73 & Hall, M., The Secret Teachings of All Ages p. LXXIX & Lillyquist, M., Sunlight & Health: The Positive and Negative Effects of the Sun on You pp. 2, 16, 19 - 21, 59, 67, 77 - 80 & Lord, S., Forever Younger Vogue Vol. 182, No. 8 Aug. 1992 p. 242 & Wills, C., The Skin We're In Discover Nov. 15, No. 11 Nov. 1994 pp. 80 - 81 & Kittles, R., Nature, origin, and variation of human pigmentation Journal of Black Studies Vol. 26, No. 1 pp. 36 - 58 & Bylinsky, G., Mass Producing Nature's Sun Screen Fortune Vol. 125, No. 11 Jun. 1, 1992 p. 131 & Mercado, J., Garcia, F., Fernandez, M., & Olivares, J., Melanin production by Rizobium melilotti GR4 is linked to nansymbiotic plasmid pRmeGR4b: cloning, sequencing, and expression of the tyrosinase gene mepA Journal of

Bacteriology Vol. 175, No. 17 - 18 Sept. 1993 pp. 5403 - 5408 & Niori, K., & Takashi, T., Gene cluster involved in Melanin biosynthesis of the filamentous fungus Alternaria alternata Journal of Bacteriology Vol. 175, No. 13 - 14 July 1993 pp. 4427 - 4429 & Schraermeyer, U., Fine structure of melanogenesis in the ink sac of Sepia officinalis Pigment Cell Research Vol. 7, No. 1 Feb. 1994 pp. 52 - 60 & Herv'e, M., Hirschinger, J., Granger, P., Deflandre, A., & Goetz, N., A 13C solid-state NMR study of the structure and auto-oxidation process of natural and synthetic melanins Biochimica Et Biophysica Acta Vol. 1204, No. 1 Jan. 11, 1994 pp. 19 - 27 & Chedekel, M., Murr, B., & Zeise, L., Melanin standard method: empirical formula Pigment Cell Research Vol. 5, No. 3 Sept. 1992 pp. 143 - 147 & Zeise, L., Murr, B., & Chedekel, M., Melanin standard method: particle description Pigment Cell Research Vol. 5, No. 3 Sept. 1992 pp. 132 - 142 & Aime, S., Fasano, M., Terreno, E., & Groombridge, C., NMR studies of melanins: characterization of a soluble melanin free acid from Sepia ink Pigment Cell Research Vol. 4, No. 5 - 6 Dec. 1991 pp. 216 - 221 & Drozdz, R., Siegrist, W., Baker, B., Chluba de Tapia, J., & Eberle, A., Melanin-concentrating hormone binding to mouse melanoma cells in vitro Febs Letters Vol. 359, No. 2 - 3 Feb. 13, 1995 pp. 199 - 202 & Valverde, P., Healy, E., Jackson, I., Rees, J., & Thody, A., Variants of the melanocyte-stimulating hormone receptor gene are associated with red hair and hair skin in humans Nature Genetics Vol. 11, No. 3 Nov. 1995 pp. 328 - 330 & Jeffery, G., Schutz, G., & Montoliu, L., Correction of abnormal pathways found with albinism by introduction of a functional tyrosinase gene in transgenic mice Developmental Biology Vol. 166, No. 2 Dec. 1994 pp. 460 - 464 & Diffey, B., Healy, E., Thody, A., & Rees, J., Melanin, melanocytes, and melanoma Lancet Vol. 346, No. 8991 - 8992 Dec. 23, 1995 p. 1713 & Chadwick, C., Potten, C., Cohen, A., & Young, A., The time of onset and duration of 5-methoxypsoralen photochemoprotection from UVR-induced DNA damage in human skin British Journal of Dermatology Vol. 131, No. 4 Oct. 1994 pp. 483 - 494 & A new ray of hope on melanoma Patient Care Vol. 30, No. 11 June 15, 1996 p. 14 & Fairview Health Services: Under Your Skin (net) & Gore, A., Earth in the Balance pp. 85 - 87 & Cancer Facts and Figures 1998 p. 4 & Melanoma FAQ (net) & Paleo Perspective . . . on Global Warming (net) The activated melanin responsible for skin color is found in the pigment layer of the epidermis (right below the stratum corneum). But as activated melanin can be found in many cells in the body, it may well be performing many functions of which scientists are presently unaware. This notwithstanding, one other interesting finding is that melanin and melantonin are crucial to the operation of the human biological clock: timing and rhythm. The term melantonin is derived from the Greek words *melas* meaning, "black" and *tosos* meaning, "workings."

Follow-up to footnote on page 9

Elamite Bowl from Mesopotamia c.2500 BCE

THE RACIALIZATION OF SLAVERY

Rogers, J.A., <u>Sex and Race</u> Vol. I, p. 151, 265 & Koch, R., <u>The Book of Signs</u> p. 18 & Clegg, R., <u>Mackey's Revised History of Freemasonry</u> & Becker, U., <u>The Continuum Encyclopedia of Symbols</u> pp. 289 - 291 & Biedermann, H., <u>Dictionary of Symbolism</u> p. 334 & Jainism, <u>A Dictionary of Comparative Religion</u> pp. 366 - 367 & Quinn, M., <u>The Swastika</u> p. 1 & Fylfot, <u>The Universal Standard Encyclopedia</u> Vol. X, p. 3558 & Jobes, G., <u>Dictionary of Mythology, Folklore and Symbols</u> p. 1517 & Goodman, F., <u>Magic Symbols</u> pp. 114 - 115

Permit me to comment briefly about the symbol today known as the <u>Swastika</u>. It is not a recent creation but actually quite old. <u>This ancient symbol had nothing to do with a particular race or hate</u>! Also known as the Fylfot, the sign was created by making four breaks in the circumference of the sun wheel (ancient emblem for the sun gods of Western Asia). The symbol's earliest use dates back to the 5th millennium BCE, and the Black peoples of Mesopotamia (see pages 8 - 11). In truth, the ancient Sanskrit words used to describe the symbol mean, "<u>Well-Being</u>." By 2000 BCE, the sign's use had migrated southward to Mohenjo-Dara in the Indus Valley. Never considered by the ancients as anything but a sign of good fortune and prosperity, it is not surprising to learn that the people of India often placed the symbol on their Buddhas. Jainists of 1st millennium BCE India, used the symbol to signify the four spheres of creation; i.e., gods, humans, animals and the underworld. Frankly, the sign is so un-European in its etymology that a century ago the German philologist Max Muller would remark: *"I do not like to use the word 'Svastika' outside of India. It is a word of Indian origin, and has its history and definite meaning in India . . ."* From India, the sign migrated east to Tibet and China where it designated good fortune, the cardinal points and infinity. The Basque of the Iberian Peninsula would also embrace the symbol. During the early centuries of Christianity in Egypt and Western Asia, followers of the way used the sign as a cryptic cross to avoid persecution by the Romans. Remarkably, the symbol was even utilized as an ancient emblem for the Black God Quezalcoatl in the New World! Finally, coming to the era of the Nazis, in actual point of fact, Hitler did not embrace the ancient swastika—merely its form. In deference here to Goodman: *"Specialists in magical symbolism distinguish between the swastika, the 'arms' of which follow the clockwise (sun-wise) direction, and the sauwastika, the 'arms' of which follow the 'widdershins' (anti-sun-wise) direction (the form the Nazis adopted)."* In closing here, from the Elamites on down, the ancients thought that if the symbol's bent arms faced to the left—the symbol possessed negative, as opposed to positive, connotations . . .

National Flag of Germany in 1933 CE

The Color Of The Curse

The Color Of The Curse

Many Westerners have used the Bible to justify racism and racial slavery. However, after touching upon the physiological benefits of possessing activated melanin—*depicting this gift as a curse seems a rather odd contradiction.* In light of this, let's take a moment to examine what the scriptures, and the ancients, actually divulged about the countenance of those who were considered divinely cursed, or unclean.

While a great deal wasn't written about the matter, what's to be found is rather interesting. When Miriam was to confront Moses about marrying a Midianite (though commonly called an Egyptian) it is explained that her condemnation was to be turned white by YHVH. In <u>Numbers</u> we read:

> "*Suddenly, Yahweh said to Moses and Aaron; 'Come all three of you, to the Tent of Meeting.' They went, all three of them,*

THE RACIALIZATION OF SLAVERY

and Yahweh came down in a pillar of cloud and stood at the entrance of the Tent. He called Aaron and Miriam and they both came forward . . . 'How then have you dared to speak against my servant Moses?' The anger of Yahweh blazed out against them. He departed, and as soon as the cloud withdrew from the Tent, there was Miriam a leper, white as snow!"[1]

The association between this color and a curse is also found in the Judeo-Christian scriptural account of Gehazi. The story tells us that

---

[1] Numbers 12:1-10 & Baltazar, E., The Dark Center pp. 146 - 147 & McCray, W., The Black Presence in the Bible p. 124 & Windsor, R., From Babylon to Timbuktu p. 24 & Zipporah, Illustrated Dictionary & Concordance of the Bible p. 1059

Some writers suggest that Miriam's objection was because Zipporah was Black; however, it is much more likely that she was troubled by the fact that Zipporah was a Midianite, and that her father Jethro was a Midianite priest. In any event, Zipporah bore Moses two sons whose names were Gershom and Eliezer.

because of Gehazi's greed, the Prophet Elisha cursed him, after which he was turned white and leprous. In <u>II Kings</u> we find the following passage: *"Naaman's leprosy will cling to you and to your descendants forever, and Gehazi left his presence a leper, white as snow . . ."*[2] Additionally, we also find white flesh being compared with the unclean state of leprosy in the Old Testament book of <u>Exodus</u>.[3]

Turning to the traditions of the ancient Christians of Africa, it is to be noted that Ethiopian Christians (*who were amongst the world's oldest*) commonly depicted the Christ and all of the disciples as black, except for Judas, whom they depicted as white. Rogers says, *"Father Fernandez, a Catholic missionary tells how the Ethiopians pictured their saints as*

---

[2] <u>II Kings</u> 5:27 & Gehazi, <u>Illustrated Dictionary & Concordance of the Bible</u> p. 383

[3] <u>Exodus</u> 4:6 & Windsor, R., <u>From Babylon to Timbuktu</u> pp. 24 - 25, 35 & Baltazar, E., <u>The Dark Center</u> pp. 146 - 147

black, and the devil as white and their God as black."

Similarly, in the Judeo-Christian teachings of the Africans of the Gold Coast we are told that in the beginning everyone was black. However, after Adam's son Cain murdered his brother Abel—God screamed at Cain so loudly that he became deathly afraid! They go on to say that it was the state of fright and guilt, that caused Cain to lose his color and become pale or white.

Frankly, ancient Easterners have long associated pale skin with misfortune and evil. For example, the 18th century Explorer Mungo Park tells us that it was deeply held by many Africans that Whites took Blacks away from Africa to eat them. Further here, as late as the 19th century, the Africans of the Mossi States believed that their land would be cursed upon the appearance of the first Whites. Williams writes:

"BEFORE THE SIXTEENTH CENTURY MOST AFRICANS ON THE continent had never seen a real white face. Since in many societies all devils and other spirits were white, the ritual to ward these off was always led by chanting dancers whose faces and bodies were hideously painted with white chalk . . ."[4]

Some may wish to portray these findings as cultural manifestations unique to Black Africa; however, it has to be noted that this sentiment was not only found in the African interior. In

---

[4] Rogers, J.A., <u>Sex and Race</u> Vol. I, p. 23, 277, Vol. II, p. 402 & Cain, <u>Illustrated Dictionary & Concordance of the Bible</u> pp. 202 - 203 & <u>Genesis</u> 4:12-14 & Donnan, E., <u>Documents Illustrative of the History of the Slave Trade to America</u> Vol. II, pp. 634 - 635 & Williams, C., <u>The Destruction of Black Civilization</u> p. 216, 243 & King, A., <u>Quotations in Black</u> p. 69

This stance on color would continue to be held by some Blacks in the West. For example, in 1884 Bishop Henry McNeal Turner would declare: *"In some places in America Black is supposed to symbolize the Devil and White symbolize God, but that is partially wrong, for the Devil is White and never was Black."*

the early Islamic World, criticisms were at times expressed about those with thin lips, thin hair, and pink (or pale) body parts in their realm. Atop that, in response to Islamic critics of Blacks in Western Asia, Amr ben Bahr (commonly known as Al-Jahiz) would declare:

> *"We, said the Blacks, have conquered the country of the Arabs as far as Mecca and have governed them . . . but you, white people have never conquered our country . . . Everyone knows that the Negroes are amongst the most generous of mortals—a quality that is found only among noble characters. Negroes are distinguished amongst other peoples by their natural gift for rhythmic dancing and the best artists on the drum, all of this without any special training. They are also the best singers . . . Negroes are physically stronger . . . A single one of them can lift stones of great weight and carry burden*

*such as several Whites could not lift or carry between them. They are brave, strong, and generous as witness their nobility and general lack of wickedness . . . Nevertheless the Slavs, for example, are greedier than the Greeks and are, at the same time less intelligent. Women and children, also, are less intelligent than men and are greedier. This proves that all the above-mentioned good traits are the gift of God, intelligence as well as goodness, generosity as well as bravery . . . The Blacks above all men have the greatest sexual desire—the man for the woman and the woman for the man. Black women are the most agreeable sexually of all women . . ."*5

---

5 Rogers, J.A., World's Great Men of Color Vol. I, pp. 163, 164 - 166, 168 - 169
Al-Jahiz is heralded as the greatest Islamic scholar of the 9th century. Of his more than 120 books, he is most noted for these: The Book of Animals, The Merit of the Turks, In Praise of Merchants and Dispraise of Officials, The Superiority in

THE RACIALIZATION OF SLAVERY

Without sanctioning any of the specifics of Al-Jahiz's assertions, it is manifest that this celebrated Moslem scholar (*and his followers*) did not view black skin as a biological trait of condemnation.[6]

Moving from Africa and Asia to Europe, Bishop makes the disclosure that many Caucasians of the Middle Ages actually underwent minor surgical procedures to make their noses and lips appear more, *not less*, prominent like Blacks.[7]

Glory of the Black Race over the White, and The Book of Eloquence and Rhetoric.
[6] Montagu, A., Man's Most Dangerous Myth: The Fallacy of Race p. 95, 99 & Malcioln, J., The African Origins of Modern Judaism p. 7 & Human Beings, Encyclopedia Americana Vol. XIV, p. 545 & Sunderland, E., Elements of Human and Social Geography pp. 59 - 60 & Coon, C., Racial Adaptations pp. 94 - 96, 97 & Montagu, A., The Concept of Race pp. 140 - 141 & Inside the Third Reich: Memoir by Albert Speer p. 73 & Rogers, J.A., Sex and Race Vol. III, pp. 146 - 148
[7] Rogers, J.A., World's Great Men of Color Vol. I, p. 169 & Bishop, M., The Horizon Book of the Middle Ages p. 246 & Milele, N., The Journey of the Songhai People p. 52 & (Video), Desmond Morris' The Human Animal: The Biology of Love 1999

Equally revealing, we even find white to be the designated color of mourning (or loss) in several parts of Europe. In deference here to Ward:

> *"White is the prevalent colour of mourning, particularly in the Far East, Ancient Rome, and Sparta. In England mourners wore white up until the Middle Ages . . ."*[8]

**Egyptian woman painted white
mourning her husband c.1400 BCE**

---

[8] Ward, P., <u>A Dictionary of Common Fallacies</u> p. 170 & Opie, I., & Tatem, M., <u>A Dictionary of Superstitions</u> p. 443 Many 20th century Europeans actually believed that to bring white flowers into someone's home was an omen of death.

The Racialization of Slavery

Needless to say, a cursory inquiry into the idea that the Old World universally considered black skin to be indicative of a "**Curse**," renders the notion dubious at best!

Ham

However, in that no single curse account has been more widely promulgated than the story of Ham—permit me to share the following about Ham being cursed by Noah. The well-known story centers on Ham (*father of the Hamites*) being cursed for not covering his naked father. Sir Godfrey Higgins most certainly had reservations about this narration (*and he was not alone*). Possessing an intellect of the first order, with the integrity to match, Higgins felt compelled to remark:

> "*There is great difficulty in settling the proper places, according to their seniority,*

*of the three sons of Noah, as all divines have allowed. I think it probable that Japheth was the <u>youngest</u>, and Ham the <u>eldest</u>, and that the story of his uncovering his father was only [later] contrived . . ."*⁹

Upon reflection, Higgins' assertion is not without some merit (in the context of race) insomuch as anthropologists worldwide explain that the African is the oldest, *not youngest*, race

---

⁹ Brackman, H., <u>The Ebb and Flow of Conflict</u> & <u>Genesis</u> 9: 18 - 27 & Higgins, G., <u>Anacalypsis</u> Vol. II, p. 361 & (Video), <u>Priestly Sins: Sex and the Church</u> 1996 & Whiston, W., <u>The Works of Flavius Josephus: Antiquities of the Jews</u> Bk. I, Chp. 6 & Japheth, <u>Illustrated Dictionary & Concordance of the Bible</u> pp. 497 - 498 & Van Sertima, I., <u>Golden Age of the Moor</u> p. 168, 362

It is put forth that Japheth's children decided to leave Asia and head northwest. During the migration, his lineage became pale and lost their language and culture. By the by, it is written that the biblically <u>cursed</u> child would be a servant. Of course, examining ancient history we eventually come to the Slavic peoples of Central Europe. It turns out that the Slavs were amongst the earliest Caucasians to come in contact with the established Black civilizations of the Southern European continent and the Mediterranean. It is also to be noted that the name of these Caucasians (Slav) is, indeed, the root word for the term "Slave."

on the earth. You see, Africa is the only continent where anthropological evidence of all of the evolutionary stages of Homo Sapien Sapien (humanity) has been found.

Briefly, the eight stages of human development are thus: (1) Australopithecus Ramidus; (2) Australopithecus Afarensis; (3) Australopithecus Africanus; (4) Australopithecus Robustus; (5) Homo Habilis; (6) Homo Erectus; (7) Homo Sapien Neandertalensis; and (8), Homo Sapien Sapien. Most telling, of these eight classifications, the only stages ever discovered outside of Africa are from the latter three catagories. In the words of Hoebel:

> *"No australopithecines have ever been found in Europe, and considering how intensively the pre-history of Europe has been explored, it is not very likely that one ever will be . . . The austraopithecines of South and East Africa are the first*

upright, bipedal hominid fossil primates consisting of two recognized species- Australopithecus africanus and Australopithecus robustus."

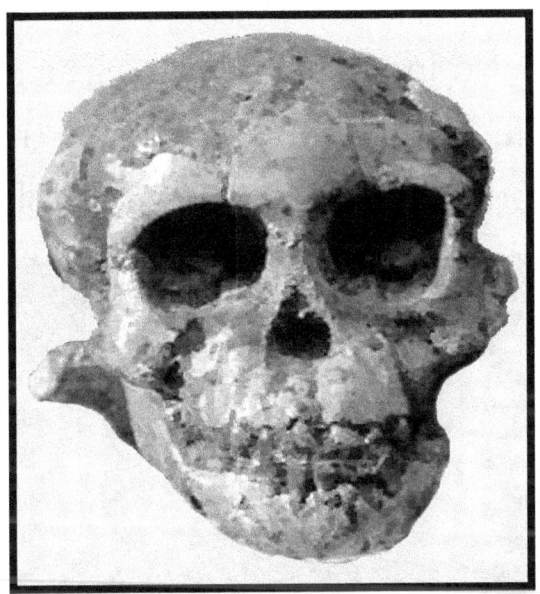

Afarensis skull found in Ethiopia[10]

---

[10] Davidson, B., Buah, F., & Ajaya, A., The Growth of African Civilization: A History of West Africa 1000 - 1800 p. 7 & Hoebel, E., Anthropology: The Study of Man pp. 136, 178 - 179 & Watson, T., Revising Human Origins U.S. World and News Report Vol. 117, No. 13 Oct. 3, 1994 p. 67 & Fischman, J., Putting Our Oldest Ancestors in their Proper Places Science Vol. 265, No. 5181 Sept. 30, 1994 pp. 2011 - 2013 & Grogan, D., & Harrison, L., Finding the Link People Weekly Vol. 42, No. 24 Dec. 12, 1994 pp. 165 - 167 & Video, The Brain: Our Universe Within 1994 & (Video),

THE RACIALIZATION OF SLAVERY

Yet, whether Higgins is partially correct, totally correct, or completely wrong about Ham—one is still left with the paradox of an incredible gift being given to someone you wish to curse; *i.e., Black people possessing the most activated melanin.* No less inexplicable, clear down into the Middle Ages we find <u>Christians throughout Europe portraying the Christ child as black</u>![11]

Our Lady of Czestochowa

<u>For the People: Interview with Dr. C.A. Diop</u> L. Middleton 1991 & Diop, C.A., <u>Civilization or Barbarism</u> p. 25
Australopithecus Afarensis dates back approximately 3.5 million years. The photo (page 41) appears courtesy of Eigene Arbeit and Wikimedia.
[11] Higgins, G., <u>Anacalypsis</u> Vol. I, p. 264, 316, Vol. II, pp. 137 - 139 & Rogers, J.A., <u>Sex and Race</u> Vol. I, p. 274
Photo of Our Lady of Czestochowa Poland (above) appears courtesy of Jim Steinhart of PlanetWare.com

Finally, there isn't any way to refute the biological fact that whatever changes transpired in human skin color—***it is clear that the transformation was from black to something else—not vice-versa***. Hence, allow me to conclude this discussion of the curse by simply reiterating the earlier pronouncement of Professor Wills:

> *"To cut a very long story short, dopaquinone follows two different routes, one leading to black and brown pigments, and the other to red and yellow pigments. The master enzyme in all this is tyrosinase. If the gene for this enzyme is defective, the result is a person with albinism, someone who makes no melanin at all. But the most remarkable discovery made by molecular biologists has been that most of us, regardless of skin color, have quite enough tyrosinase in our melanoctes to make us very black. In*

those of us with light skin, something is preventing the enzyme from functioning at full capacity . . ."[12]

Albino girl with family in New Guinea

---

[12] Diop, C.A., <u>The African Origin of Civilization: Myth Or Reality</u> p. xv & Lemonick, M., <u>Everyone's Genealogical Mother: Biologists Speculate "Eve" lived in Sub-Saharan Africa</u> Time Vol. 129, No. 4 Jan. 26, 1987 p. 66 & Lewin, R., & Foley, R., <u>Principles of Human Evolution</u> & Rogers, J.A., <u>Sex and Race</u> Vol. I, pp. 29 - 30 & Wills, C., <u>The Skin We're In</u> Discover Nov. 15, No. 11 Nov. 1994 pp. 79 - 80 Photo appears courtesy of GNU-F.D.L. version 1.2. For an explanation of albinism see pages 18 and 22.

CAUCASIAN ENSLAVEMENT THROUGH THE AGES

THE RACIALIZATION OF SLAVERY

Throughout world history, peoples of all lands and races have undergone the predicament of slavery. As Keller was to remark: *"There is no king who has not a slave among his ancestors, and no slave who has not had a king among his!"*

New Kingdom Egyptian Pharaoh victorious over Indo-Europeans c. 1400 BCE - Portrait housed in the British Museum – London England

Despite this well-known historical fact, Western educators (and media) arduously portray slavery as a circumstance exclusive to the Black Race.[1] This is actually rather incredible considering that the very term "*slave*," is derived from the word, Slav (one of the earliest designations for the Caucasian). To quote Padilla, "*The word 'slave' itself and its various Western cognates (esclavo, schiavo, sklava, etc.) is derived from that ethnic group which was the most numerous external group in the medieval Mediterranean slave trade, the Slavs.*"[2]

Caucasian Enslavement

Nomenclature notwithstanding, in that it has become so fashionable in the West to

---

[1] One can't help but be reminded of Orwell (see page ix).
[2] Davidoff, H., The Pocket Book of Quotations p. 171 & Simon, L., Iberia and the Mediterranean World of the Middle Ages p. 389 & Rogers, J.A., Sex and Race Vol. I, p. 29

Africanize the experience of slavery—let's examine what academics divulge about enslavement and the Caucasian Race—because facts do not vanish, even when they've been ignored:

> Diop explains that Caucasians could be found amongst the slave ranks of the Egyptians by the time of Rameses II.
>
> Heurgon tells us that ancient Caucasians of the regions of Greece and Gaul made up a substantial portion of the slave class of the Etruscans who were Black.

Bust of Etruscan woman c. 500 BCE

Caucasian Enslavement

Most of the population of ancient Greece carried the slave status. Cox makes the disclosure that of Athens' 600,000 people, 10,000 males had full citizenship and the rest of the men were slaves. Of course, Greek women had no rights, to speak of, at all. Gouldner writes:

"Greek uneasiness about slavery probably arose not only because all were potential victims but also from the manner in which slaves were 'recruited.' While slaves were often 'barbarians,' that is, non-Greeks, coming perhaps especially from Thrace, the lands around the Black Sea, Asia Minor, and the Levant, nonetheless, Greeks also enslaved Greeks, particularly so with the increasing bitterness of their intercity wars during the late fifth and fourth centuries. Slaves were in large measure won in war..."

In Simons' <u>Barbarian Europe</u> we read:
"In their more mundane dealings with the empire, the Germanic tribesmen were more fortunate. Enterprising Roman merchants had long been sending north gaudy jewelry suited to barbarian tastes, agricultural implements and household

THE RACIALIZATION OF SLAVERY

wares, wines to vary the tribal fare of curdled milk and home-brewed beer, and coins, which many Germanic warriors valued as ornaments rather than as currency. The Germans had one important commodity to offer in exchange, human beings—the captives they took in their internecine wars. Traders herded these prized chattels south and sold them into servitude as gladiators, domestic servants and held hands. Among them were thousands of Slavs—men, women and children—seized by the Germans in forays against the weaker tribes of northeastern Europe. In time, so many of these hapless people were toiling in captivity that their ethnic name, which meant 'glorious' to them, passed into common usage as the inglorious 'slave.'"

Ancient Roman Coins

Caucasian Enslavement

In Bede's celebrated history, the English youth who were taken to Rome are summarily identified as slaves.

So that we're clear, White slavery was not just undertaken in Southern European—it was widely practiced in the northern regions as well. Owen states:
"Slavery was a common institution among the Germanic peoples of the Iron Age, as it was among the Romans and the peoples of the Near East. The slaves were acquired by purchase or captives of war . . . The slaves were used for both domestic and farm labor . . ."

Interesting findings are made when we investigate Druid history. Scullard shares the following:
"According to Caesar, Gaulish [French] society was divided into three groups: the Druids, the warrior aristocracy . . . and the common people. The Druids who were in fact drawn from the warrior class, ranked highest. They were priests who controlled all public and private sacrifices, which might include human victims, and they judged nearly all disputes . . . The rest

THE RACIALIZATION OF SLAVERY

of the people consisted largely of free cultivators, but the condition of many must have been wretched, some sinking to serfdom or even slavery."

It must be noted that state powers were not the only entities to deal in human flesh. In deference here to Robinson:
"Evidence is available from several sources to show that at the end of the sixth century Jewish slave-dealers were in the habit of selling in Italy and elsewhere slaves obtained from Gaul or Britain. In a letter which Gregory wrote to a priest in Gaul named Candidus in 595, he bids him to spend some money due to himself in redeeming English slaves who might afterwards be trained to become monks. He further expresses a wish that these youths should be sent to Rome accompanied by a priest who was to baptize them in case they became ill and were likely to die."

Moving into the era of the Moors, we again encounter the enslavement of Caucasians. Malcioln maintains:

Caucasian Enslavement

"The eighth century, after the Christian era, experienced African-Arab domination from Algeciras, the seaport at the southern tip of Spain, to the Pyrenees frontier between France and Spain. Of interest to historians is the fact that the Arab Dynasty in Spain was made up of Africans from Morocco, many Slavs, Austrians, and Germans. And the only free men among these converts and seekers of spoils were the Africans. The other warriors were all bought from Charlemagne and his successors as slaves . . ."

The ensuing passage is found in Van Sertima's, <u>The Golden Age of the Moor</u>:
"Amidst the beauty and wealth, a socio-political plague was spreading: 'Jews who had been slaves now began trading in slaves.' According to T. B. Irving, between the years of 786 and 1009, 'Franks and Jews traded Slavs and Germans who had been taken prisoner . . . on the Frankish territories. Thus "slav" and "slave" became interchangeable [terms] . . . They [the Franks and Jews] made young boys into eunuchs at Verdun . . . The slaves were driven from France to Spain in great

THE RACIALIZATION OF SLAVERY

herds like cattle. When they reached their destination, the men were purchased as servants or laborers, the women as household help or concubines . . .' This practice was not exclusive to Spain; W. E. B. DuBois notes that during the 16th century 'the Mohammedan rulers of Egypt were buying white slaves by the tens of thousands in Europe and Asia and bringing them to Syria, Palestine and the Valley of the Nile.'"

Portion of the Alhambra built by the Moors in Spain

Permit me to take a moment to make one point here about Islamic slavery. In the Islamic realm, race was never a determining factor. In the words of Padilla:

"It is important to address the issue of ethnicity and slavery. While blacks are indeed encountered in the documentation, Mediterranean slavery was primarily a matter of religion and had little to do with race. Muslims enslaved Christians and Christians enslaved Muslims . . . Ibn Khordahbeh wrote, as early as the ninth century, that it was through the Western Mediterranean that slaves of Slavic, Roman, Frankish and Lombard origin were transported, he especially notes that it was a source for Roman and Spanish female slaves."

Continuing further west, Anderson has divulged the fact that the Scots enslaved many Englishmen during the Middle Ages.

We also find slavery being practiced in feudal England. Howarth writes:
"There were no slaves in little estates like Horstede. There was a large number in

THE RACIALIZATION OF SLAVERY

England, but they worked in the households and demesnes of the rich and powerful . . . it was possible to buy a slave in any town, and their value can be guessed from the purchase tax that was paid . . . If a horse was sold, the buyer and seller each paid a penny in tax, and if a man was sold they each paid four pence."

Finally here, Rogers would make this disclosure about Caucasian enslavement in Britain:

"The English upper class of the eleventh century treated white women of the lower class in a manner that reminds one of how their descendants, the Virginian colonists, treated black women. William of Malmesbury, English historian of the twelfth century, tells how the nobles used 'to sell their female servants when pregnant and after they had satisfied their lust either to public prostitution or foreign slavery.' He tells of another noblewoman who used to buy up the most beautiful slave girls and sell them at a profit in Denmark. When the Normans ruled England they regarded the Anglo-Saxons, a whiter complexioned people than they,

CAUCASIAN ENSLAVEMENT

in the same manner as the American slaveholders regarded the Negroes . . ."[3]

---

[3] Diop, C.A., The African Origin of Civilization: Myth Or Reality p. 218 & Tarn, W., Hellenistic Civilization & Heurgon, J., Daily Life of the Etruscans pp. 67 - 70 & Cox, G., African Civilizations and Empires p. 110 & Keller, W., The Etruscans pp. 244 - 245 & Gouldner, A., The Hellenic World pp. 28 - 29 & Simons, G., Barbarian Europe p. 18 & Owen, F., The Germanic People p. 150 & Scullard, H., Roman Britain p. 16 & Robinson, C., Conversion of Europe pp. 98 - 99 & Jews in Europe: Before 900, Dictionary of the Middle Ages p. 85 & Malcioln, J., The African Origins of Modern Judaism p. 201 & De Graft-Johnson, J., African Glory p. 74 & Van Sertima, I., Golden Age of the Moor p. 168, 362 & Simon, L., Iberia and the Mediterranean World of the Middle Ages pp. 389 - 390 & Windsor, R., From Babylon to Timbuktu p. 37 & Rogers, J.A., Sex and Race Vol. III, pp. 4 - 5, 8 & Howarth, D., 1066: The Year of the Conquest p. 17 & Wood, M., Doomsday: A Search for the Roots of England p. 60 - 61 & Briggs, A., A Social History of England & Richardson, H., & Sayles, G., The Governance of Mediaeval England p. 52 & Anderson, A., Scottish Annals

Levant was a word that was used to signify the lands of the Eastern Mediterranean Sea coast. Incidentally, Bill Veith explains that every fiat currency in history has lost its value, save that of its intrinsic character: *notes are paper*. It is also noteworthy that Medieval laws against unions between people of different religions were strictly enforced in Europe—especially, Catholics and non-Catholics. Prohibitions were also enforced against English and Irish marriage. Here are some examples of marriages that were forbidden by state law as late as the 20th century: Christian and non-Christian Serbians; heathens and atheists with Christians in Sweden; Moslems and Jews in Persia and Morocco; and, Whites and other races—in Germany (1935 - 1945), South Africa (1949 - 1985) and parts of the U.S.A. until 1967.

The Portuguese Enter Africa

The Portuguese Enter Africa

With the 15th century decline of the Moors on the Iberian Peninsula, the Portuguese would begin to set their sights on the African continent. Historians explain that incited by the wondrous tales of Moslem chroniclers, the Portuguese were eager to explore the coast of West Africa. Additionally, after the capture of Ceuta (in North Africa) from the Moroccans, Portugal's Prince Henry actually had a staging ground from where he could launch his forces. Jones writes:

> *"Under his direction, the Portuguese navy moved steadily down the coast. They settled Madeira in 1419 and the Azores in 1439 . . . in 1444, they colonized the Cape Verde Islands to use as a trading base . . . They pressed on, reaching the coast of present-day Sierra Leone in 1460 . . . Once past the equator, the Portuguese found what they had been looking for: gold. Along the Gold Coast of West Africa, they*

came upon wealthy gold - trading empires . . . Seeking to protect their discovery from competitors, the Portuguese court secured orders from the pope . . . granting Portugal possession of all the territory it 'discovered.'"[1]

1. Portugal
2. Spain
3. Ceuta
4. France
5. Greece
6. England
7. Netherlands
8. Rome

---

[1] Van Sertima, I., <u>The Golden Age of the Moor</u> p. 352 & Jones, C., <u>Africa: 1500 - 1900</u> pp. 10 - 11 & Davidson, B., <u>Africa in History</u> pp. 175 - 178 & Williams, C., <u>The Destruction of Black Civilization</u> pp. 245 - 260 & Blake, W., <u>History of Slavery and the Slave Trade</u> p. 23 & Donnan, E., <u>Documents Illustrative of the History of the Slave Trade to America</u> Vol. II, pp. xviii - xix

The Portuguese Enter Africa

Obviously, the hierarchy of the Catholic Church had no right to cede these prosperous and self-sufficient African kingdoms to the Portuguese; yet, that is precisely what their *holy* certification set in motion. Accordingly, Pope Alexander VI issued a Papal Bull barring Spain from entering Africa. The decree was enacted to stop the martial skirmishes that were taking place between Portuguese and Spanish sailors on Africa's Gold Coast. As recompense to the Spaniards, Alexander ceded the territories of the New World to them.[2]

Spain notwithstanding, the Machiavellian plan of the Portuguese and Catholic Church in Africa was threefold: (1), to secure for themselves access to the continent's gold; (2), to thwart Islam's influence in Africa as much as possible; and (3), to control Africans by converting them

---

[2] Diggs, E., Black Chronology p. 41

to Roman Catholicism. In Chancellor Williams' <u>The Destruction of Black Civilization</u> it is explained:

> "The idea was to unite the Christian forces of Europe with Africa in an all-out war against the Arabs . . . The Portuguese, however, did not reach the African Christian kingdom at the time they sought it for the promotion of their campaign against Islam. They had therefore begun the work of creating a Black Christian kingdom in their own image. This was Kongo. By 1512 no one needed to guess or speculate about the Portuguese plans . . . Manuel, made them clear in documentary form: <u>The Regimento</u>. This is one of the interesting and significant documents in the history of black people because it was the first detailed blue print for the conquest of the black man's mind

The Portuguese Enter Africa

(acculturation via Christianity), his body (slavery), and his country."[3]

The Regimento was clearly an extension of the Mudejar policy employed against the Moors of Iberia: under the auspicious of Roman Catholic brotherhood and salvation—millions of Africans were led into perpetual servitude.[4] In the eyewitness narrative of James Barbot we find:

"The Portuguese also cause the slave they ship off to be baptiz'd, it being forbid under pain of excommunication to carry any to Brazil, that are not christened. However, it is pitiful to see how they croud those poor wretches, six hundred and fifty

---

[3] Williams, C., The Destruction of Black Civilization pp. 250 - 251
The Portuguese did not take into account the fact that the lines of religion were not as rigidly established in Africa as Europe. For instance, the kingdom of Abyssinia was led by Christian Arabs and Black Christian Hebrews. Hence, every Arab was not a Moslem and every Hebrew did not practice Judaism (*problematic environs for the* divide and rule *ploy*).
[4] Harvey, L., Islamic Spain: 1250 to 1500

THE RACIALIZATION OF SLAVERY

> *or seven hundred in a ship, the men standing in the hold ty'd to stakes, the women between decks, and those that are with child in the great cabin, and the children in the steeridge, which in that hot climate occasions an intolerable stench. The voyage is generally perform'd in thirty or thirty-five days, the trade-wind carrying them . . ."*[5]

Likewise, the 18th century chronicler C.B. Wadstrom would make these observations about Catholicism and the trade:

> "Great numbers of slaves who come from the remote inland countries, are shipped from Congo, Angola, etc. None, however . . . are sent as slaves to the Brazils, except black convicts; and even these, before they are put on board, are catechised and

---

[5] Donnan, E., Documents Illustrative of the History of the Slave Trade to America Vol. I, p. 459

The Portuguese Enter Africa

receive baptism, a rite which has been found to console their minds under their unhappy circumstances . . . the sailors are chiefly blacks, called Negros Ladinos, who speak their language, and whose business it is to comfort and attend the poor people on the voyage . . ."[6]

It must not go without mention that many of Portugal's largest dealers in human cargo were Catholic priests. What's more, many of these

---

[6] Donnan, E., Documents Illustrative of the History of the Slave Trade to America Vol. II, p. 618 & Aptheker, H., American Slave Revolts p. 163

Even with these measures, by 1526 the first successful slave revolt had been undertaken by Africans in North America. Aptheker says, *"The first settlement within the present borders of the United States to contain Negro slaves was the locale of the first slave revolt."* The Spanish founded a colony near the mouth of the Pedee River (South Carolina) with 500 Whites and 100 Blacks. After the colony had experienced months of hardship (mainly due to uncontrollable circumstances) the Blacks seized the opportunity to rebel. Unable to fight the Blacks and run the colony, the Whites left for Haiti. The remaining Africans were welcomed by, and joined with, the Native Americans of the region.

THE RACIALIZATION OF SLAVERY

priests are known to have possessed large African harems. Of the Kongo it was written:

"Priests were not only among the leading slave traders, but they also owned slave ships . . . Priests also had their harems of black girls, some having as many as twenty each. They were called 'house servants' by these 'holy fathers.'"[7]

So, the 16th century ushers in the brainwashing of millions of Africans in the East and West by the Catholic Church. Of a sudden, the spiritually adept African could not hope to reach heaven, if

---

[7] Williams, C., The Destruction of Black Civilization p. 253 & Lacy, D., The Abolitionists p. 81
In all honesty, Catholic clergymen were not the only clerics guilty of such behavior. For example, the 19th century American abolitionist Stephen Foster relates: *"The American church and clergy, as a body, were thieves, adulterers, man stealers, pirates and murderers . . . the Methodist Episcopal Church was more corrupt and profligate than any house of ill fame in the city of New York . . . the southern ministers were desirous of perpetuating slavery for the purpose of supplying themselves with concubines from among the hapless victims and that many of our clergymen were guilty of enormities that would disgrace an Algerine pirate!"*

he did not first accept Roman Catholicism. And this despite these historical facts: the Messiah was not a Roman Catholic; the Christ did not speak Latin; the oldest surviving Christian texts were authored in Egypt, not Rome; and the faith's earliest defenders were Black![8]

Shackles worn by enslaved Africans c. 1600 CE

Atop this, the dynamic history and culture of the African were mocked and maligned—while lesser achievements, relatively speaking, of the White oppressor were exaggerated and celebrated. For instance, ancient Egypt had 31 royal dynasties; *in truth, many of those dynasties were longer than the Caucasian's control of the Iberian*

---

[8] Worthy, R., YHSVH pp. 148 - 151

THE RACIALIZATION OF SLAVERY

Peninsula at that time.[9] Yet, the former never happened—the latter colossal.

<u>From name changes, to proscriptions on education and learning about African culture, to the erosion of the unilateral authority of African royalty—the colonization of the African mind was ubiquitous and based wholly upon the castigation of historical truth!</u>[10] Add the fact that slavers mandated that their ministers fallaciously pervert Christian teaching to convince generations of brutalized Africans that

---

[9] Waddell, W., <u>Manetho</u> & Budge, E.A., <u>Egypt</u> & Gardiner, A., <u>Egypt of the Pharaohs</u> & Budge, E.A., <u>A History of Egypt</u>

[10] Williams, C., <u>The Destruction of Black Civilization</u> p. 249 & Hallett, R., <u>Africa Since 1875</u> p. 434 & Milele, N., <u>The Journey of the Songhai People</u> p. 45

Deferring here to Williams: *"As the 15th century moved on towards the 19th, the Europeans became less and less 'white devils' and more and more white masters, backed up by awesome firepower. 'White' was no longer the face of evil in the Black world. It had changed places with 'black.' Now 'black' was the badge of evil . . ."* An illustration of the success of the Portuguese stratagem in Africa is evidenced by the fact that by 1906—the army of the Belgian Congo consisted of 16,000 African soldiers who were completely subservient to 360 Europeans.

The Portuguese Enter Africa

it was a Caucasian Christ's will that they be enslaved—and it is understandable why Western education and religion are sore subjects for many people of African heritage today...

Lastly, the use of religion by governments to achieve some worldly aim was nothing new (*nor have they stopped*).[11] However, the perversion of the faith by people who have never known the Messiah must not be conjoined with the Christ, or the followers of His way: *don't continue to be hoodwinked, <u>it's Chess—not Checkers</u>!* In deference here to Chesterton: *"The Christian ideal has not been tried and found wanting. It has been found difficult; and left untried."*[12]

---

[11] Worthy, R., <u>The Founders Façade: Christianity, Democracy, Freemasonry, and the founding of America</u>

[12] Elkins, S., <u>Slavery</u> p. 60 & Augarde, T., <u>The Oxford Dictionary of Modern Quotations</u> p. 52

For example, it is often said that organized religion has killed more people than any other institution in history—*wrong!* <u>The rulers of nation states have "*distorted and used organized religion,*" to justify killing more people in history than anything else available to them.</u>

Spain & The New World

Spain & The New World

One of the consequences of Columbus' so-called discovery of the New World would be to increase Spain's need for manpower. The first prosperous commercial crop of the Spanish in the New World was sugar cane. In that Pope Alexander had ceded Africa to the Portuguese, he also sanctioned their trading enough Africans to the Spanish to fulfill this demand for manpower. Hence, the early impetus, and facilitation, of the Slave Trade in the New World.[1]

Truth be told, Africans were not the only slaves of the Spanish in the New World. Spain's first move was to enslave the Native American.

---

[1] Diggs, E., <u>Black Chronology</u> pp. 41 - 42 & Davidson, B., <u>Africa in History</u> pp. 175 - 176 & <u>Chronicle of America</u> p. 42

By the 1470s, the Portuguese had begun trafficking about a thousand West Africans a year to Lisbon. The first sugar cane plantations were established on the Island of Hispaniola (Santo Domingo of modern day Dominican Republic) in 1493. In the coming years, the Spanish would refine their molasses (a sugar by-product) and produce rum.

THE RACIALIZATION OF SLAVERY

Naturally, the serfs and slaves of the feudal states of Western Europe did not suddenly disappear with the coming of the 16th century. Chroniclers explain that many Caucasian slaves were regularly transported to the Americas. As a matter of fact, in 1501, the governor of Spanish America, Nicolas de Ovando, would formally object to the importation of any more African slaves because they often rebelled and fled. After escaping, the Africans commonly joined with Native American tribes in the outlying areas. To thwart this, a special license was issued from Medina del Camo to Ojeda in 1504, <u>for the importation of White slaves only</u>. This measure totally halted the transport of African slaves to the Western hemisphere.

During the ensuing years, a number of free and captive Blacks would cross the Atlantic with the Spanish: for example, in 1505 Ovando sought to use a small number of Blacks in the copper mines of Hispaniola; in 1508, some African slaves worked in mines in the West Indies; in 1510, Blacks arrived in Puerto Rico with Micer Geron; in 1512, Blacks were transported to Cuba from Spain; and, dozens of free Blacks would accompany Balboa and Cortez on their exploratory missions. However, the most pivotal event in the process of racializing slavery in the Americas occurred in 1516.

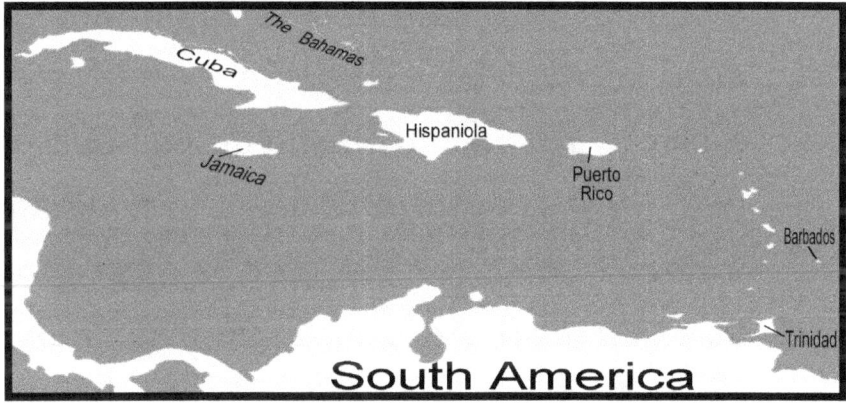

In 1516, Spain's King Charles I issued a dictum that would not merely reverse Ovando, but inveterate the use of the African as slave labor in the Americas. Remarkably, it appears that the

The Racialization of Slavery

impetus for Charles' decree was Dominican opposition to the enslavement of the Native American. A Spanish news article of 1518 states:

> "Seeking to quiet Dominican protests over Indian slavery, King Carlos I has granted an 'asiento de Negros,' the first European monopoly for the importation of African slaves to the Indies. The Dominican conscience awoke in 1511 on Hispaniola following Fray Antonio de Montesinos's fiery sermon opposing the encomienda system. Young Bartolome de Las Casas, who in 1510 became the first priest ordained in the New World, has since taken up the cause... after his ordination, he witnessed a routine 'pacification' mission in Cuba. Led by Captain Panfilo do Narvaez, it turned into a massacre: 'There was a river of blood, as if a multitude of cows had been slaughtered.'"

Inasmuch as Las Casas was so vehemently opposed to Native American slavery—it is incredible that he should be so callous about the enslavement of Africans. The article continues:

> *"To meet labor needs, Las Casas turned to the Africans, who have proved stoic under adverse conditions in southern Iberia and the Canary Islands. Negroes have been going to the Indies as servants since 1502. It is hoped that mass importation will relieve the labor burden borne by the Indians..."*[2]

---

[2] Diggs, E., Black Chronology pp. 41 - 42, 44, 46 - 48 & Sloan, I., The Blacks in America 1492 - 1977 p. 1 & Toppin, E., Biographical History of Blacks in America Since 1528 & Espanola, Merriam Webster's Geographical Dictionary p. 487 & Hispaniola, Columbia Lippincott Gazetteer p. 789 & Charles I, The World Book Encyclopedia Vol. III, pp. 380 - 381 & Chronicle of America p. 22 & Donnan, E., Documents Illustrative of the History of the Slave Trade to America Vol. I, p. 15 & Rogers, J.A., Sex and Race Vol. II, p. 399 & Lynch, J., Spain: 1516 - 1598 p. 217 & Mencken, H., A New Dictionary of Quotations p. 1108

Charles V (Hapsburg) inherited the Spanish crown from his grandparents Ferdinand and Isabella. Upon his coronation in 1516, he became Charles I of Spain. In 1519, Charles succeeded his other grandfather Maximilian I as Emperor of

The Racialization of Slavery

Charles' edict would have profound ramifications upon the racialization of slavery in the West. Even though it, *justly*, freed the Native American from subjugation—*for the first time a "kingdom mandate" specifically targeted a single race for generational subjugation!*

The Africanization of Spanish slavery in the New World officially began in 1517. Ellen Diggs writes, *"The Emperor Charles V granted a charter to a Flemish [Dutch] merchant for the exclusive importation of African slaves into Spanish America, thus, definitely founding the slave trade . . ."*[3] These admissions leave little

---

the Holy Roman Empire (German-based kingdom of Central Europe). The Spanish would eventually decree: *"No Indian may be reduced to slavery, whether for making war, for rebellion or for any other reason, and no one shall work an Indian as a servant or in any other capacity against his will."* Of course, the error of referring to the Native American as Indian, stems from the fact that Columbus thought that he had landed in India. The term West Indies is yet another example of this. But instead of correcting the error, we find his inaccurate terminology continuing to be used to this day.
[3] Diggs, E., Black Chronology p. 48

wonder as to why William Blake should remark: *"Britons and Scythians were the fellow slaves of the Ethiopian: But at last all the other Nations of the Earth seemed to conspire against the Negro Race."*[4]

Charles V of the Holy Roman Empire c. 1548

---

[4] Blake, W., <u>History of Slavery and the Slave Trade</u> pp. 93 - 94 & Windsor, R., <u>From Babylon to Timbuktu</u> p. 20
Windsor says, *"The Scythians included all the wandering tribes who dwelt mostly near the north of the Black and Caspian seas. They were regarded by the ancients as tremendously lacking in intelligence and civilization."*
Portrait of Charles by Sustris - courtesy of The Yorck Project.

The Hues Of Slavery In North America

The Hues Of Slavery

Allow me to point out that even with the ratification of the African Slave trade by the Spanish in the 16th century, the racialization of slavery in North America was neither immediate, nor unassailable. Although seldom discussed, many of the Africans who crossed the Atlantic after 1516 were not thrust into permanent bondage—and every Caucasian was not necessarily exempt from lifelong enslavement.

For example, the very first Africans to be received in the British colonies were not slaves, but explorers and indentured servants—many eventually becoming landowners in North America. A Jamestown newspaper article of 1619 entitled, <u>Dutch ship brings 20 Africans to be sold</u>, reported the following:

"'There came in a Dutch man-of-warre that sold us 20 negars,' reports settler John Rolfe. Welcomed by the English

The Racialization of Slavery

colonists as a useful addition to the labor force, these Africans, the first to be brought to the settlement, are indentured servants, in return for their passage to America, have agreed to serve for a period of five years. When that time is completed, they may buy land and, in general act as full citizens of Jamestown . . . It is not known whether the African immigrants have freely consented to these terms. Of these newly arrived immigrants, 15 have been purchased to serve for Sir George Yardley, the Governor of Virginia. Yardley is owner of the 1000 acre Flowerdew Hundred plantation . . . Since one of the goals of the Jamestown colony is to make full use of the resources of the land, and turn a profit as quickly as possible . . . It will, therefore, be no surprise if more Africans are transported to the colony."

The Hues Of Slavery

Despite the early stance of the colonies, by 1641 the indentured servitude policy towards Africans was ended at the insistence of the British crown. The reason for the reversal was the tremendous income that England was beginning to receive from the North American colonies: profits being wholly generated by the uncompensated labor of enslaved Africans.[1]

Continuing well on into the era of racially sanctioned slavery in America, *while there can be no doubt that the overwhelming majority of captives were African—chroniclers make the disclosure that countless numbers of Whites were enslaved in North America as well!* The distinguished Elizabeth Donnan and J.A. Rogers provide the ensuing passages:

---

[1] Haynes, R., Blacks in White America Before 1865 & (Video), Tear on the Face of America Brown 1986 & Chronicle of America p. 51, 71 & Hornsby, A., Chronology of African American History pp. 2 - 3
Massachusetts was the first colony to sanction slavery in North America.

The Racialization of Slavery

In 1698, leaders of the colony of South Carolina wanted to enact legislation to begin trafficking Caucasian slaves. The <u>Act For The Encouragement Of The Importation Of White Servants</u>, stated:

"Whereas, the great number of negroes which of late have been imported into this Colony [South Carolina] may endanger the safety thereof if speedy care be not taken and encouragement given for the importation of white servants . . . And be it further enacted, that every owner of every plantation to which doth belong six men negro slaves above sixteen years old, shall take from the Receiver one [White] servant, when it shall happen to be his lot to have one, and shall within three months pay the Receiver so much money for the said servant as the Receiver gave to the person from whom he received the same; and the owner of every plantation to

which doth belong twelve negro men, as aforesaid, shall when it shall be his lot, take two [White] servants as aforesaid; and every master of every plantation proportionately."

"James Annesley, son and heir of Lord Altham of England was 'sent into America and sold there as a common slave' for thirteen years."

"In 1791, William Cunningham confessed . . . in August 1774, that he had brought in a number of white people, kidnapped in Ireland and sold them into slavery in America. When these Europeans arrived young it was easy to sell them as Negroes, the more so as when they were kidnapped, they had no papers or proof of whom they were . . ."

The Racialization of Slavery

"In some instances whites of the South sell their children to traders; the practice of kidnapping white children and transferring them southward is said to be notoriously on the increase . . ."

"Jacobs quotes further from <u>The Independence</u> of Jamestown, Wisconsin, on the sale of white orphans, 'The price of each slave was $10 cash.' He quotes other advertisements . . . 'four thousand of such children have been sold' and that 'fifty will be sold every two months.'"

It should also be noted that laws preventing Blacks from buying Whites, were not enacted until 1670 in the North American colonies:
"Tobacco and cotton were needed in Virginia for sale to Europe. Tobacco was at one time currency in Virginia. White

serfs were growing it . . . Fifty-one years after the Negro's arrival in Virginia, a law was passed to prevent his buying white people. Louisiana passed such a law as late as 1818."

"The <u>Abbeville Banner</u> of Alabama tells of one James C. Wilson who married a white woman, and later sold both her children to a preacher, named Guilford, as slaves. Later, he sold his wife's fifteen year old brother as a slave, too."

"An article from the Cincinnati Philanthropist . . . tells of the sale of a white woman, who was sold as a Negro, and her ten children by her two white masters."

"The case of Salome Mueller is the best known instance of a white person held as

THE RACIALIZATION OF SLAVERY

a Negro . . . Salome, or Sally, was born in Alsace, Germany, July 10, 1813, and was brought to America in 1817 by her father, who was sold into indentured servitude. On the voyage across her mother died, and soon after reaching America, her father also died. Sally was in some way separated from the remainder of the family, and fell into the hands of Fritz J. Miller, a slave-dealer, who seemed to have specialized in the business of selling kidnapped white people as Negroes. Miller hired her to Belmonti, a cafe proprietor of New Orleans. Several witnesses testified on the stand that Miller had other 'Negro slaves as white in color and features as Sally.' Twenty-four years passed. Sally, now called Mary Bridget, was married to a Negro slave, by whom she had three children. In the meantime Sally's uncle, George Mueller, had been searching everywhere for her. Then one day, one of Sally's cousins who had come over on the ship with her passed Belmonti's cafe, and saw a woman scrubbing the steps. Struck by the Mueller resemblance, she asked the woman if she wasn't Sally Mueller, white. 'No,' said Sally, 'I'm a yellow girl, named Mary Bridget.' Unconvinced, the cousin persisted, 'Do you have two hair moles about the size of a coffee-bean on the inside of each of your thighs about midway up from the knee?' Sally said she had. And then the long fight for Sally's freedom. A careful examination of Sally's figure, form, features, color, and hair revealed no trace of the African. She had long, straight black hair, hazel eyes, Roman nose, and thin lips. Her face and neck were dark from work in the fields, but underneath her clothing she was as white as any other white person. The court, however, ruled that she was a Negro. Her friends took the case to the Supreme Court of Louisiana. That also decided against her. Then a German resident in New Orleans went to her birthplace in Alsace, dug up her birth certificate, brought it back and she was freed."

In actual point of fact, the argument for the enslavement of poor Whites was openly expressed by the upper crust during the 19th century in America:

"One fact that militated against the poor white man held as a Negro was the belief that poor whites were better off as slaves, a doctrine whose principal supporter was George Fitzhugh, a leading writer of the times. William Chambers of encyclopedia fame who visited America in the 1850's . . .

quoted Fitzhugh as follows: 'Race! Do not speak to us of race—we care nothing of breed or color. What we contend for is, that slavery whether of black or white, is a normal, a proper institution in society.' 'So proclaim Southern writers in the United States,' observes Chambers, 'The principle of enslaving only colored person . . . is now antiquated and a scheme which embraces slavery of every race and variety of complexion is at length put forward as a national and desirable arrangement for all parties—a highly commendable state of things . . . <u>If slavery is to be at all vindicated it must not now be on the narrow basis of color but on the broad grounds that there is an inherent right in the stronger and more wealthy classes to reduce the poorer, and it may be, more ignorant orders to a state of perpetual bondage.</u>'"

The Racialization of Slavery

Atop the fact that a countless number of Whites were outright slaves in America—I would be remiss not to address the matter of those persons of interracial heritage. In 1664 a Maryland news article called, <u>Children of Negroes doomed to slavery</u> explained:

"In the latest of a series of laws dealing with slaves, Maryland has proclaimed the marriage of English women to Negro slaves a disgrace to the nation and has ruled that any children from such a marriage be given over to slavery. Virginia enacted the first law acknowledging slavery as an institution in 1660..."

However, children of mixed race were most often considered to be the race of the mother. This practice was initiated, primarily, so that White slaveholders could legally keep the children that they sired with Black women enslaved. Children of White fathers and interracial (Black and White) mothers were commonly deemed White. Obviously, as children of interracial parentage come in all shades, shapes and sizes—many passed completely undetected into White society. It is to be noted that Thomas Jefferson, Alexander Hamilton, Andrew Jackson, Abraham Lincoln and Hannibal Hamlin would all face allegations of interracial ancestry. What's more, Washington and Jefferson were widely accused of fathering children with Black women by their contemporaries. But to move from accusation to fact—after testing the DNA of descendants of Jefferson and Sally Hemings—geneticists have concluded that Jefferson did have at least one child with his biracial paramour. To Quote Dr. Eugene Foster, *"I can't say it seals it—but*

THE RACIALIZATION OF SLAVERY

it's very, very, very likely." Truth be told, ethnologists surmise that as many as one out of every ten Whites from the Southern United States has at least one African ancestor.[2]

It is manifest that every African was not a slave and every Caucasian was not free. Thus, the matter is actually deeper than race; *understand, the focus of the lower brain is destruction and consumption—the higher, life and creation.* Should one dare to examine the tree and the

---

[2] Donnan, E., Documents Illustrative of the History of the Slave Trade to America Vol. IV, p. 250 & Rogers, J.A., Sex and Race Vol. I, p. 25, Vol. II, pp. 208 - 213, 401 & Jenkins, W., Pro-Slavery thought in the Old South p. 304 & (Video), Tear on the Face of America Brown 1986 & Hornsby, A., Chronology of African American History p. 3 & Chronicle of America p. 71, 112, 345, 362 & Rogers, J.A., The Five Negro Presidents pp. 3, 5 - 11, 14 - 18 & Brodie, F., Thomas Jefferson: An Intimate History pp. 216, 228 - 245, 350 - 351 & Chang, K., Jefferson Fathered Slave Son ABCNEWS.com (net) & (Video), Oprah Winfrey: White Relatives Meet Black Relatives Harpo 1995 & Ross, R., The Elite Serial Killers of Lincoln, JFK, RFK & MLK pp. 248 - 254 While we're on the subject, a compelling argument has even been made about the interracial heritage of J. Edgar Hoover.

millennial plight of the majority of Caucasians in Western Europe, here is what's found:

> *"For one thousand or more years—the Middle Ages—Europe was one huge slave camp, the largest slave camp in history. Europe was then a feudal state ruled by the Church. The rulers were insignificant in numbers while the rest of the population were serfs and villeins. Anybody with even a smack of education knows that villeinage and serfdom were forms of slavery. Europeans should therefore be the last people to denounce others as descendants of slaves . . ."*[3]

In closing, allow me to explain that despite being inundated with visions of the virtuous and law abiding European noble—*historical fact does*

---

[3] Cox, G., <u>African Empires and Civilizations</u> pp. 170 - 171
A villein was a person who was under the control of his lord but free in his relations with other men. Serfs were essentially slaves who could not be sold away from a particular plot of land.

THE RACIALIZATION OF SLAVERY

not square with that representation. You see, the main avenues of income for nobles was their take of the agricultural output of the subsistence farming serfs and peasants on their lands—and pillaging (robbing) the lords, and defenseless, of other lands. For instance, Davis writes: *"The French court was convulsed with mirth 'to hear the Duke of Lorraine describe how he and his men raided villages, ravishing, torturing, and killing every woman, old women included.'"* Incidents of this sort occurred in Europe far more than most wish to acknowledge.[4]

No less revealing, rather for defense or plunder, the fighting man was a staple of feudal Europe. Yet, despite being responsible for his lord's life and property—<u>many knights were not deemed free men by nobles</u>. In Germany, France and Normandy, the terms <u>vassal</u> and <u>knight</u>, were analogous to perpetual *"servant"* and *"slave."*[5]

---

[4] Davis, E., The First Sex pp. 253 - 254
It is noteworthy that such events even provide the backdrop for von Eshenbach's Parzival and the Holy Grail legend.
[5] Notestein, W.,   The English People on the Eve of

THE HUES OF SLAVERY

Medieval depiction of a 15th century knight

Colonization: 1603 - 1630 pp. 13 – 15 & (Video), The Western Tradition: The Middle Ages Annenburg 1989 & Hoyt, R., Life and Thought in the Middle Ages pp. 55 - 58 & Hudson, H., The Story of the Renaissance p. 5 & Davis, C., Western Awakening Vol. II, p. 7, 11 & Anderson, A., Scottish Annals & Butler, S., Speech on Interventionism (net)

Five hundred years later, it's incredible how little has changed. In the words of Smedley Darlington Butler, Major General - United States Marine Corps: *"There isn't a trick in the racketeering bag that the military gang is blind to. It has its 'finger men' to point out enemies, its 'muscle men' to destroy enemies, its 'brain men' to plan war preparations, and a 'Big Boss' Super-Nationalistic-Capitalism. It may seem odd for me, a military man to adopt such a comparison. Truthfulness compels me to. I spent thirty-three years and four months in active military service as a member of this country's most agile military force, the Marine Corps. I served in all commissioned ranks from Second Lieutenant to Major-General. And during that period, I spent most of my time being a high class muscle-man for Big Business, for Wall Street and for the Bankers. In short, I was a racketeer, a gangster for capitalism."* Portrait of knight (above) appears courtesy of The Library of Congress – Concilium zu Constanz

The 16th Century Advent Of The Negro

The Advent Of The Negro

One of the principal devices for creating confusion in the minds of Africans in the West has been racial, and cultural, misidentification. Just as the Spanish were to demean the African character of the Moors and create new labels for them like Mudejars and Moriscos in Europe—they would give new names to the African captives that they transported to the New World.

Portrait of a Moor in Europe c. 1600 CE

THE RACIALIZATION OF SLAVERY

Forasmuch as the Spanish and Portuguese were mindful of the martial threat that the Islamic World represented—and also aware of the cultural prowess of the kingdoms of Africa—such designations as <u>Moor</u>, <u>Morisco</u>, or even the ancient and widely used <u>Ethiopian</u>, would not suffice: evoking the historic and accomplished. **NO**! <u>The naming program for these new African captives had to not only wipe out their personal identity, it also had to be a racial designation that could not muster the slightest hint of their historical identity and heritage</u>!

Accordingly, the thrust of the 16th century acculturation program for these brutalized and displaced people centered on <u>forbidding the use of their native names and language—the total denial of African history—and an immersion in the Roman Catholic religion</u>. Along with this assault on the African psyche, a brand new racial appellation was also assigned to them: **Negro**.

THE ADVENT OF THE NEGRO

G.K. Osei observes, *"With the introduction of [African] slavery into Spain and Portugal in the fifteenth century the Spanish 'Negro' from the Latin 'Niger' [often thought to mean] (black) generally superseded 'Moor' [North African]."*[1]

Insomuch as many of these newly created Negroes were the descendants of many African societies—the deployment of such a blanket classification was most guileful. Obviously, these Africans possessed various hues and features as they came from many tribes and regions. What's more, this African population was not a cultural monolith any more than every

---

[1] Cox, G., African Empires and Civilizations pp. 169 - 170 & Windsor, R., From Babylon to Timbuktu p. 21 & Brooks, L., Great Civilizations of Ancient Africa p. 23
Of course, the Spanish term negro means, *"black."* So that there will be no confusion, allow me to briefly comment about the later use of the word negro by English slavers. The Anglo-Saxons already had a term that possessed the exact same meaning as the Spanish word negro: black. However, they simply chose to embrace the earlier nondescript terminology and stratagems of the Spanish.

THE RACIALIZATION OF SLAVERY

Caucasian is Polish. Over and above that, these Africans' acceptance of the Spanish term would eventually lead to a form of psychosis; i.e., *an artificial mental disassociation between their selves and their ancestors and homeland.*

These measures were not undertaken by happenstance. Slave traffickers long held that people taken captive, but kept in a close proximity to their homelands, would struggle to obtain their freedom. Conversely, people who believed they were a great distance from their homelands were more likely to become resigned to their circumstance and resist less. Daring not leave anything to chance, the Portuguese and Spanish were not content to merely distance the flesh—they sought to create devices to distance the mind's eye as well: *you must be Negroes and no more than the little we say that means!*[2]

---

[2] Donnan, E., Documents Illustrative of the History of the Slave Trade to America Vol. II, pp. 633 - 634

THE ADVENT OF THE NEGRO

Frankly, the word Negro does not begin to describe the African any more accurately than the term Pale-face (as in the Native American's, "*Pale-face speaks with forked tongue*") identifies every Caucasian. Thus, the vehement objection to the (*land-less and culture-less*) word Negro, as a racial designation, by many conscious people of African heritage. In Black Names in America: Origins and Usage we find:

> "*Names have been used not only to identify a human being but also to vilify, depersonalize and dehumanize. Sam and Sambo, which Dr. Puckett identifies as common slave names of the seventeenth century, became racial slurs in the twentieth century when black men were commonly summoned by these names. The social significance of names is also*

Hence, the need for the **Slave Codes** and miseducation: you cannot read and write; you cannot marry; and, you cannot assemble. Without life affirming instruction, humans can be reduced to little more than *monkey see—monkey do . . .*

THE RACIALIZATION OF SLAVERY

manifested in summoning forms such as 'boy' or 'nigger' which supplanted the use of a name. The psychic impact was to reduce one to the level of a stereotype or non-person..."[3]

Nigger

Briefly, in that the term <u>Nigger</u> is commonly used to malign the character of the Black Race, permit me to bring some historical perspective to this word. For starters, the need to castigate people with activated melanin was not conspicuous in the cultures of the Old World—*it's late*. That said, historians often encounter the term <u>Niger</u> in ancient chronicles; yet, having less to do with skin color, per-se, than locale. In deference here to Rogers:

---

[3] Puckett, N., <u>Black Names in America: Origins and Usage</u> p. v

The Advent of the Negro

"Rome, like Egypt and Greece, had no color distinctions. Her extensive literature reveals none. Rome's attempt at a color-line begins with Mussolini thousands of years later. Peoples of all races and colors were brought to Rome . . . Sudanese, Ethiopians, Egyptians, Moors, Greeks, Parthians, Gauls, Celts, Belgians, Saxons, Britons and thrown into a vast melting pot. We find proof of the absence of color prejudice in the word, Niger . . . The word comes from the River Niger, and Nigritae means the people from the River Niger. 'Ni' probably means 'great' and Ger, or Geir, is African for river. At first Niger had nothing to do with black than the waters of the river itself . . . Some of the most illustrious Romans bore the surname 'Niger.'"[4]

---

[4] Rogers, J.A., <u>Sex and Race</u> Vol. I, p. 86, Vol. III, p. 4 & Snowden, F., <u>Blacks in Antiquity</u> p. 169

Rogers is spot on here as a countless number of memorable Romans bore the surnames <u>Niger</u> and <u>Africanus</u>. An example of the former is the accomplished, Pescennius Niger—the latter, the celebrated Black Roman Emperor, Lucius Septimius Severus Africanus, who ruled the empire brilliantly from 193 - 211 CE.

Emperor Lucius Septimus Severus c. 200 CE

The Advent of the Negro

The Severus Dynasty ran from 193 - 235 CE. A tribute to Lucius Septimius Severus Africanus by Cassius Dio (a contemporary) reads as follows:

> *"He was a small man, but physically strong . . . His mind was extremely keen and vigorous. He did not get as much of an education as he wanted, and because of this he was a man of few words, although he had plenty of ideas. He did not forget his friends. His enemies he treated with a very heavy hand. He took a great deal of thought over all his plans; but he never gave a thought to what was said about him . . . and he met all necessary expenditures unstintingly . . ."*[5]

---

[5] Warmington, B., <u>The North African Provinces</u> & Soames, J., <u>The Coast of Barbary</u> & Grant, M., <u>The Roman Emperors</u> & De Graft-Johnson, J., <u>African Glory</u> & Collingwood, R.G., <u>Roman Britain</u> & Birley, A., <u>Septimius Severus: The African Emperor</u> pp. 198 - 199

The Romans commemorated this African Emperor with the Triumphal Arch of Lucius Septimius Severus in the Roman Forum. The arch was built in 203 CE. Septimius Severus photo (Berlin Tondo) appears courtesy Antikensammlung, Staatliche Museen Zu Berlin - Preussischer Kulturbesitz.

THE RACIALIZATION OF SLAVERY

Obviously, there isn't anything in the historical etymology of the word Niger (Great River) to warrant the disparagement of Africans. But even if a river could somehow be negatively portrayed, and then morphed into a human character flaw—all of the Africans who were brought to America were not natives of the Niger River region; i.e., people being transported by slavers from as far east as Madagascar.

In 1681, correspondence between traffickers and the Royal African Company went thus:

> *"Wee are apprehensive the Trade that is of Late drove to Maddagascar for negroes ... And it is noe small quantities have been imported being between 900 and 1000 that have been brought and sold here in about 2 mo'th time..."*[6]

---

[6] Donnan, E., Documents Illustrative of the History of the Slave Trade to America Vol. I, p. 130, 274 & Mannix, D., Black Cargoes p. 246

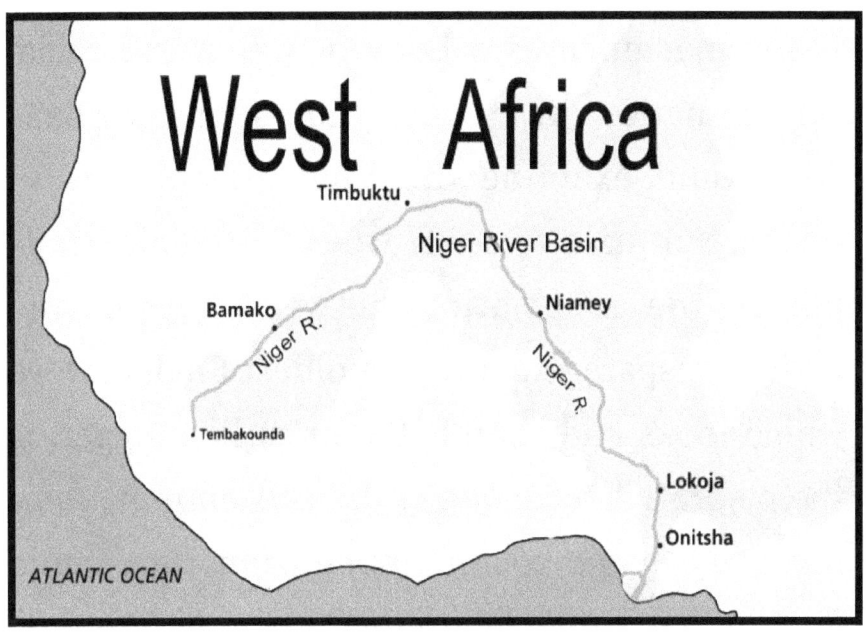
Niger River Basin

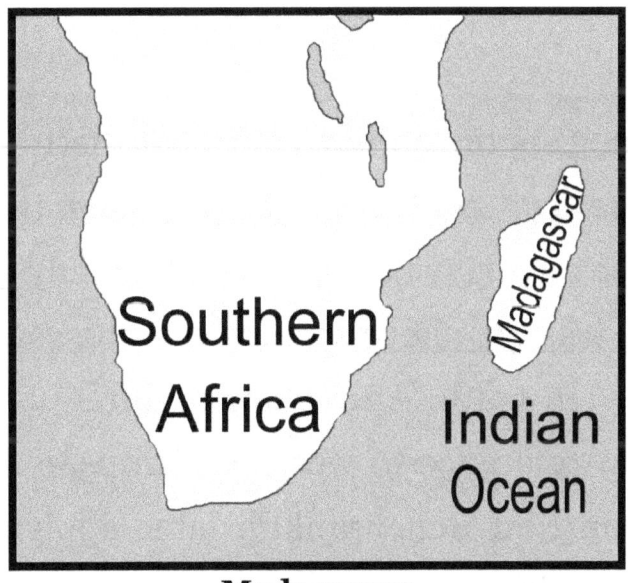
Madagascar

THE RACIALIZATION OF SLAVERY

Now, inasmuch as a body of water and racial condemnation are hardly synonymous, perhaps we should examine the English language of recent centuries to see if we can etymologically justify the association between <u>nigger</u> and African disparagement. The oldest English word which looks and sounds the most like nigger, is the pejorative term <u>Niggard</u>. *But hmmm', once more we come to an appellation that could hardly be properly applied to a kidnapped, brutalized, and unjustly maligned people of any color.*

Etymologists trace the term to Northern Europe and the 14th century. <u>It was used there to describe anyone who was greedy, unduly selfish, or who was not above stealing the possessions of others</u>. In truth, Anglo-Saxons often used the word in reference to wealthy European misers. We even find Ben Franklin later applying the term to White colonists in Pennsylvania, when admonishing them for their callous and duplicitous treatment of the Native American. This statement is found in Franklin's, <u>Writings</u>:

> "*One Hundred and Forty peaceable 'Indians' yet remain in this Government. They have, by Christian Missionaries, been brought over to a 'Liking,' at least, of our Religion; some of them left their Nation which is now at War with us . . . to shew their Confidence in us, and to give us an equal Confidence in them, they have brought and put into our Hands their Wives and Children. Others have lived long among us in 'Northampton' County, and most of their Children have been born there. These are all now trembling for their Lives. They have been hurried from Place to Place for Safety, now concealed in Corners, then sent out of the Province, refused a Passage through a neighboring Colony, and returned, not unkindly*

perhaps, but disgracefully, on our Hands. 'O Pennsylvania!' once renowned for Kindness to Strangers, shall the Clamors of a few mean Niggards about the Expense of this 'Publick Hospitality,' an Expense that will not cost the noisy Wretches 'Sixpense' a Piece . . . force you to turn out of your Doors these unhappy Guests . . . Those whom you have disarmed to satisfy groundless Suspicions, will you leave them exposed to the armed Madmen of your Country?—Unmanly Men! who are not ashamed to come with Weapons against the Unarmed, to use the Sword against Women, and the Bayonet against young children; and who have already given such bloody Proofs of their inhumanity and Cruelty . . ."[7]

---

[7] Rosen, R., A Short History of Charleston p. 64 & Writings: Franklin p. 557

Clearly, Franklin was not addressing a single African in his remarks. But, to demonstrate just how completely void of race the actual English etymology is, let me share this brief exchange between Antipholus and Dromio in William Shakespeare's, <u>The Comedy of Errors</u>. In Act 2 Scene 2 we find:

> Dromio: *There's no time for a man to recover his hair that grows bald by nature.*
> Antipholus: *May he not do it by fine and recovery?*
> Dromio: *Yes, to pay a fine for a periwig and recover the lost hair of another man.*
> Antipholus: *Why is Time such a niggard of hair, being, as it is, so plentiful an excrement?*[8]

---

[8] The Complete Works of William Shakespeare (net)

The Racialization of Slavery

So, etymologically speaking, how do we get from money-grubbing Caucasians in Europe to the blanket condemnation of a historically accomplished actively melanized population in North America? <u>Nothing more than ignorance, malice, and opportunity</u>.

Linguists explain that the Anglo-Saxon slavers who first trafficked Africans with the Spanish, simply pronounced the word Negro as <u>Negar</u>. Over time, negar has germinated down many different corridors; however, its earliest use was to simply signify the color black, as in, *"What color was her coat? It was negro."* Laughable to think that negro, or negar, could encapsulate the character of the progeny of such historically accomplished Africans as the Ewe, Fante, Efik, Ibebio, Yoruba, Dogon, Twi, Kongo, Mandinka, Moors, Nubians, Ethiopians, and so forth![9]

---

[9] Hornsby, A., <u>Chronology of African American History</u> p. xiii & Davis, E., <u>The First Sex</u> p. 124 & Rosen, R., <u>A Short</u>

Look, no journey—*be it short or far, or by force or consent*—can change the racial, or ethnic, identity of a people. Thus, it is obvious that the purpose of the designation was, *and for that matter still is*, to imprison the African mind in the realm of the "**Indoctri-Niggated**": *heads I win, tails you lose . . .*

FYI: the ancient Chinese believed that wisdom began with calling things by their right names.[10] Hence, it is a shame that so much weight continues to be given to words that, in fact, mean so little. In that our lives depend on the lies we reject and the truth we accept—please hear this ancient African proverb: *It is not what someone else calls you that matters—What matters is that to which you answer . . .*[11]

History of Charleston p. 65 & Milele, N., The Journey of the Songhai People p. 214 & Jackson, P., When Roots Die & Stuckey, S., Slave Culture p. 12
[10] Seldes, G., The Great Quotations p. 678
[11] Brown, T., Black Lies, White Lies p. 121 & Akbar, N., Chains and Images of Psychological Slavery

Black In The Old World

THE COLOR BLACK

In these later ages, Westerners have spared no effort to make the color black (negro in Spanish) synonymous with malevolence. The artifice most often used is to make no distinction between some evil (or offensive) deed and this color verbally. Although the entire list of these idioms is too long to list here—permit me to touch upon a few of the most commonly used expressions:

Black Death –
{The Bubonic Plague, which occurred in Europe during the Middle Ages}

Black Hearted –
{A person who has a wicked heart or poor morals}

Blackmail –
{A threat to expose secret information about someone if they will not pay to keep it confidential}

Black Eye –
{A phrase used to impart disparagement}

Black Hat –
{Black hats are only worn by the bad guys}

Black Market –
{The underground, or illegal, economy}

The Racialization of Slavery

Black Cat –
{Black cats are evil and you don't want one of them to cross your path}

Black Monday —
{Commonly used to refer to stock market crash on October 19, 1987. In actual point of fact, Black Monday, Tuesday and Thursday all refer to stock market crashes.

Dark Ages –
{An epoch of Caucasian history in Europe of little culture and achievement}

Dark Horse —
{Something that has little chance of becoming a champion}

Black Comedy –
{Humor often-surrounding death or some obscenity}

Black Cloud —
{Imparts impending danger or doom}

It's either Black or White —
{Something that's either hated or loved}

Black Ops —
{Secret government operations such as kidnapping, extortion, subversion, and assassination}

Black Sites —
{Secret bases where Western governments send the people they kidnap to be imprisoned and/or tortured}

Even though these phrases seem innocuous, the overarching implication is clearly imprinted in the mind of every Westerner. While I'm not sure that Sigmund Freud himself could fathom the compulsion to obfuscate the truth in this way—have you ever noticed that many of history's "**_Blackest_**" deeds, were committed by its admittedly "**_Whitest_**" people?

Black In the Past

Forasmuch as the peoples of the Old World saw black in a much different light, I'd like to touch upon some of the attitudes of the ancients about this color. In truth, the people of the forefront did not associate black with negative or unfortunate events. Quite the opposite, black was the personification of many positive attributes! For instance:

THE RACIALIZATION OF SLAVERY

The French Egyptologist R. A. S. De Lubicz explains that the ancients considered black to be the color of the beginning and the completion of cycles.

Reeves tells us that black was synonymous with the spiritual rebirth in some cultures.

Many saw black as the color of fertility, boldness, durability and victory.

Ancient astrologers associated the color with the planet Saturn.

In the realm of amulets, black stones were seen as possessing the power to protect wearers from evil.

Gaskell explains that the widely treasured and mysterious substance of the alchemist was black in color.

Early Christians saw black as the color of the world and gold as the color that symbolized those who obtained the spiritual rebirth!

In European heraldry, it was black that was the color of constancy, prudence and wisdom.

We even find Shakespeare commenting in his <u>The Two Gentlemen of Verona</u>: *"Black men are pearls in beauteous ladies' eyes."* Frankly, objective students of the history of Europe during the Middle Ages are hard pressed to find fault with the assessment that the expression, tall, dark and handsome, meant exactly that—*"<u>Tall, dark and handsome</u>."*[1]

---

[1] De Lubicz, R., <u>Sacred Science: The King of Pharaonic Theocracy</u> pp. 201 - 202 & Reeves, N., <u>Into the Mummy's Tomb</u> p. 47 & Rogers, J.A., <u>World's Great Men of Color</u> Vol. I, p. 168 & Waddell, W., <u>Manetho, Ptolemy</u> p. 193 & Budge, E.A., <u>Amulets and Talismans</u> pp. 326, 424 - 425, 487 & Roger, J.A., <u>Sex and Race</u> Vol. III, pp. 134, 137 - 139 & Gaskell, G., <u>Dictionary of all Scriptures and Myths</u> p. 38 & <u>The Lost Books of the Bible and the Forgotten Books of Eden</u> p. 211 & Windsor, R., <u>From Babylon To Timbuktu</u> p. 24 & Baltazar, E., <u>The Dark Center</u> p. 146 & Boorstin, D., <u>The Discoverers</u> p. 95 & Budge, E.A., <u>Osiris: The Egyptian Religion of Resurrection</u> Vol. I, p. 324 & Butzer, C. (Ed.), <u>Ancient Egypt: Discovering Its Splendors</u> p. 196 & Ward, P., <u>A Dictionary of Common Fallacies</u> & Opie, I., & Tatem, M., <u>A Dictionary of Superstitions</u> p. 443

If the truth is to be told, the color of condemnation for many First World cultures was not black—but white (see The Color Of The Curse).

Finally, in light of the fact that dark faces are so often associated with beasts and monsters in these times—allow me to close by explaining that for thousands of years (*on the continents of Africa, Asia and Europe*) the face of the most benevolent, and redeeming, principle in creation was black! In fact, academics have made many comparisons between this Black figure, Osiris, and the later arriving Messiah of the Christians.[2]

---

[2] Budge, E.A., The Book of the Dead p. 53, 98, 118, 425 & Lurker, M., The Gods and Symbols of Ancient Egypt & Muller, M., Mythology of All Races Vol. XII pp. 113 - 120 & Higgins, G., Anacalypsis Vol. II & Sykes, E., Everyman's Dictionary of Non-classical Mythology pp. 162 - 164 & Baptism, Encyclopedia of Religion Vol. II, p. 60 & Hall, M., The Secret Teachings of All Ages p. CLXXXIII & Pike, A., Morals and Dogma of the Ancient and Accepted Scottish Rite of Freemasonry pp. 295 - 296 & Murphy, E., Diodorus on Egypt & Budge, E.A., Osiris: The Egyptian Religion of Resurrection Vol. I, p. 2, 167

Just as the Christians believe that the Christ overcame death, the earlier Egyptians ascribed this feat to Osiris; i.e., the first entity to be reborn in creation. Osiris also oversaw the entry of righteous souls into heaven and the eternal destruction of the wicked. In truth, many cultures were to celebrate Osiris. The Greeks explained that one of his first acts was to deliver mankind from all manner of bestial and destructive living. He also gave laws and spirituality to mankind.

The Color Black

Osiris

The Transatlantic Trafficking Of Human Beings

The Transatlantic Trafficking Of Humans

The centuries of West African history that roughly correspond to Europe's <u>Dark Ages</u> were hardly backward or barbarous. Indeed, these centuries would give rise to a <u>Golden Age</u> on the continent for several kingdoms. This period's West African societies were well governed, highly cultured, and materially prosperous—from Mali, to Songhay, to Benin, to Zimbabwe, to the Mossi States! However, that African prosperity and stability would eventually fall prey to the designs of the European.

In short, a number of Africa's rulers, unwisely, embraced the duplicitous counsel of merchants *who did not have their best interest at heart*. Of course, the most tragic consequence of that error was the facilitation of the transatlantic trade. This marks the beginning of the use of the African as nothing more than a commodity: <u>*life reduced to a material resource for generations*</u>.

The Racialization of Slavery

Scores of Africans tightly chained together naked in a Portuguese slave ship c.1830 - NavioNegreiro

There isn't any question that the inhumanity of slavery in the Western hemisphere began at the moment the man, woman, or child was captured in Africa. The 17th century chronicle of John Barbot provides us with eyewitness testimony of transactions between Europe's slave traffickers and the dealers in Africa:

> *"The rate in trade is generally adjusted with the king, and none permitted to buy or sell till that is proclaimed; whereby he reserves to himself the preference in all dealings, he for the most part having the*

greatest number of slaves, which are sold at a set price, the women a fourth or a fifth cheaper than the men. This done, and the king's customs paid, as above mentioned, the factor has full liberty to trade, which is proclaimed throughout the country by the king's cryer . . . This regulation being agreed on by the king and factors, the goods are brought ashore, and carried on men's backs to the French house, whither the king himself repairs, or else sends his factors or agents. When he has chosen what he thinks fit, the nobility or prime persons pick out what they have occasion for, and after them every other Black; and then every buyer, king or subject, pays the factor the number of slaves, according to the amount of the goods each of them has so pitched upon. As the slaves come down to Fida from the inland country, they are put into a booth, or prison, built for that

THE RACIALIZATION OF SLAVERY

purpose, near the beach, all of them together; and when the Europeans are to receive them, they are brought out into a large plain, where the surgeons examine every part of every one of them, to the smallest member, men and women being all stark naked. Such as are allowed good and sound, are set on one side, and the others by themselves; which slaves so rejected are there called Mackrons, being above thirty five years of age, or defective in their limbs, eyes or teeth; or grown grey . . . These being so set aside, each of the others, which have passed as good, is marked on the breast, with a red-hot iron, imprinting the mark of the French, English, or Dutch companies, that so each nation may distinguish their own, and to prevent their being chang'd by the natives for worst, as they are apt enough to do . . . The branded slaves, after this, are returned to their former booth, where the factor is to subsist them at his own charge . . . There they continue sometimes ten or fifteen days, till the sea is still enough to send them aboard . . . Before they enter the canoes, or come out of the booth, their former Black masters strip them of every rag they have, without distinction of men or women; to supply which, in orderly ships, each of them as they come aboard is allowed a piece of canvas, to wrap around their waist . . . in the aforesaid months of January, February and March, which are the good season, ships are for the most part soon dispatched, if there be a good number of slaves at hand; so that they need not stay above four weeks for their cargo, and sometimes it is done in a fortnight [14 day period]. The Blacks of Fida are so expeditious at this trade of slaves, that they can deliver a thousand

THE RACIALIZATION OF SLAVERY

every month . . . As to the slaves, and the trade of them, whereof I have before spoke at large, it will be proper to observe here, that commonly the slaves we purchase at Fida and Ardra, are brought down to the coast from several countries, two and three hundred leagues up the inland: where the inhabitants are lusty, strong, and very laborious people: thence it is, that tho' they are not so black and fine to look at as the North-Guinea and Gold-Coast Blacks, yet are they fitter for the American plantations, than any others; especially in the sugar islands . . . One thing is to be taken notice of by sea-faring men, that these Fida and Ardra slaves are of all the others, the most apt to revolt aboard ships, by a conspiracy carried on amongst themselves; especially such as are brought down to Fida, from very remote inland countries, who easily draw

THE TRANSATLANTIC TRAFFICKING OF HUMANS

others into their plot . . . and will therefore watch all opportunities to deliver themselves, by assaulting a ship's crew, and murdering them all, if possible: whereof, we have almost every year some instances, in one European ship or other, that is filled with slaves . . ."[1]

During the 16th century, the Portuguese, Spanish, French, English, Danish and Dutch participated in the African slave trade. By the 1640s, the Brandenburgers, Swedes, Genoese and some European Jews of Western Europe

---

[1] Davidson, B., Buah, F., & Ajaya, A., The Growth of African Civilization: A History of West Africa 1000 - 1800 pp. 118 - 127, 159 - 160 & Davidson, B., The Lost Cities of Africa p. 93 & Dubois, F., Timbuctoo the Mysterious p. 285 & Benin City, Collier's Encyclopedia Vol. IV, p. 57 & Benin, The Encyclopedia Britannica Vol. II, p. 102 & Donnan, E., Documents Illustrative of the History of the Slave Trade to America Vol. I, pp. 292 - 295 & League, Merriam Webster's Deluxe Dictionary p. 1043
The distance of a league can vary from 2.4 to 4.6 statute miles; thus, Barbot is describing locales anywhere from 240 to 1400 miles inland.

THE RACIALIZATION OF SLAVERY

had become transatlantic traffickers of human beings as well.

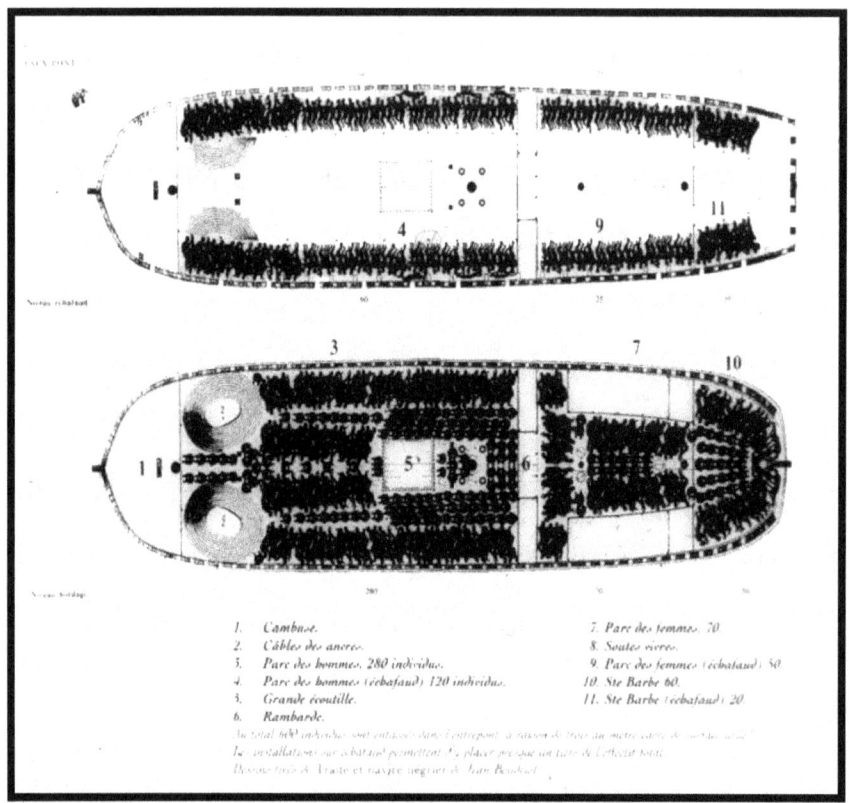

Diagram of French ship loaded with 600 Africans in 1784

In the ensuing years, slave ships from the North American colonies would be sent to Africa. A Boston news article of 1645 entitled, <u>First slaving ships sent from America</u>, states:

"The profitable but unpleasant trade of slaving has become an American industry with ships now frequently leaving Boston harbor for raids along the West African coast. There, natives are captured or purchased by the Americans and taken to Barbados, where they are traded for salt, tobacco, sugar and wine. These valuable commodities are sold at a huge profit. In fact, the profits have been so great as to encourage the continuance and growth of this trade in the North American ports. The market in Barbados ships slaves to colonies throughout the Americas."[2]

---

[2] Donnan, E., Documents Illustrative of the History of the Slave Trade to America Vol. II, p. xiii, 51, 117 & Faber, E., Jews, Slaves, and the Slave Trade pp. 16 - 17 & Chronicle of America p. 65, 95, 99 & Duignan, P., & Clendenen, C., The United States and the African Slave Trade 1619 - 1862 p. 9 & The Suppressed Book About Slavery pp. 121 - 158
Decades later, another Boston news account would explain, Triangular trade is thriving, from molasses to rum to slaves: "American ingenuity has developed a clever way of redressing the unfavorable balance of trade with England . . . it is known as 'three-cornered trade,' the 'round about' or,

The Racialization of Slavery

Though exchange rates fluctuated, one captain explained that African males were obtained for 130 gallons of rum, women for 110 gallons of rum, and children for 80 gallons of rum. Once in the West, children were commonly sold for hundreds of dollars, while the price for healthy adults ranged between one and two thousand.

Estimates of the total number of Africans transported across the Atlantic have been placed anywhere from the ridiculously low figure of 3.5 million to the probably slightly inflated number of 25 million. W.E.B. Du Bois places the number of Africans to <u>survive</u> the transatlantic crossing at about 15,000,000. While we may never know the actual tally, it is clear that the main destination of these people was the Caribbean.

---

most commonly, 'triangular trade' . . . There are many variations on this pattern. A brigantine, for instance, will leave Newport with a cargo of rum and iron, sail to Africa and trade that cargo for slaves, then transport the slaves to Barbados, where they are exchanged for molasses and sugar, then proceed home . . ."

To quote Shapiro, "*Historically, the Caribbean area was the centre of the slave traffic . . .*"[3]

A statistic that's often disputed is the African mortality rate during these transatlantic voyages. Tightly packed together—*with little care for ventilation and for hygiene*—the documentation suggests that millions of Africans would die before even reaching the New World. Although no one has definitive statistics, mortality rates for Africans on slave ships were recorded anywhere from about 12% on French ships (under the best of conditions) to as high as 55% on some Dutch vessels (under the worst). A colonial news article of 1772 reported:

> "*Figures obtained from slave ships indicate that an increasing number of slaves are dying en route to America from Africa. This is believed to be the result of*

---

[3] Curtin, P., The Atlantic Slave Trade: A Census p. 13 & Shapiro, H., Race Mixture pp. 16 - 17

THE RACIALIZATION OF SLAVERY

> *overcrowding, lack of hygiene and generally poor care provided by the slave traders..."*[4]

Additionally here, the trafficking of Africans also cost many White crewmembers their lives: <u>scholars place the figure as high as one out of every five seamen</u>. Further, the price of this trade to the Caucasian would not end there. James Rawley makes the following observation:

> *"A closer look at the mortality of white persons in Africa confirms the saying that Africa was the 'white man's grave.' Employees of the Royal African Company for the years 1684 to 1732 suffered an appalling loss which doubtless would have discouraged recruits had they known the grim story. A recent study starkly concluded that <u>three out of five Europeans</u>*

---

[4] Curtin, P., <u>The Atlantic Slave Trade: A Census</u> pp. 275 - 276, 286 & <u>Chronicle of America</u> p. 137

The Transatlantic Trafficking Of Humans

<u>stationed in Africa died during the first year</u> ... K.G. Davies saw no certainty that more than 10 percent returned to England."[5]

Ports of Call

At this late date, it is practically impossible to definitively determine the African homeland of every Black person in the Americas. Frankly, there are a myriad of reasons for this: (1), though a ship might have secured 600 people from a particular coastal kingdom, there is a high probability that the majority of those individuals were obtained from a warring (or subject) region further inland; (2), there isn't any guarantee that the registry of every trafficker was accurate; (3), African names and tribal

---

[5] Rawley, J., <u>The Transatlantic Slave Trade: A History</u> pp. 285 - 286

The Racialization of Slavery

distinctions were not noted; (4), many of these ledgers have been lost, hidden, and/or destroyed; (5), the resale (or reintroduction) of enslaved Africans from one colony (and/or nation) to another is one more impediment; and (6), the fact that the generational preservation of their African past by the majority of the captives was practically non-existent—all work to make this an incredibly difficult endeavor. *Indeed, the foresight of Kunta Kinte to tell his daughter the story of his past—and Kizzy's determination to keep it alive in her children—culminating in the odyssey of Alex Haley and his book "Roots," was akin to catching lightning in a bottle!*

This all notwithstanding, from the volumes of records that have survived, historians have been able to ascertain that the African regions most instrumental in trafficking humans across the Atlantic were the coastal lands from the Senegal River to Southern Angola. Thomas writes:

> *"From early on, different Europeans had set up their regular establishments in Africa. The Dutch, the English, and then the French had their trading places, especially in the region of the rivers Senegal and Gambia and on the Gold Coast."*[6]

Here is further testimony from eyewitnesses about the African lands most implicated in the transatlantic trade:

> Portugal's Edward Lopes said of the Congo: *"There is also a greater trafficke and market for slaves, that are brought out of Angola, then in any place else. For there are yearly brought by the Portugais above 5000 head of Negroes, which afterwards they conveigh away with them, and so sell them into divers [various] parts of the world . . ."*

---

[6] Thomas, H., The Slave Trade p. 388

THE RACIALIZATION OF SLAVERY

James Barbot wrote of 18th century Angola:

"The chiefest trade of the Portuguese and other whites [in Congo] consist in slaves, carried thence to several ports in the West Indies, to work in the Sugar mills, and in the mines, the Europeans not being sufficient for that labour; and no men can do it so well as these Angolans for a time: and thus it is at the expense of the lives of these poor wretches, that we draw such vast wealth from America. It is affirm'd that when the Spaniards were masters of Portugal, they transported every year fifteen thousand slaves out of Angola, into the new world. The Portuguese still transport a very great number."

Most of the Africans that the Danes brought to the New World were also from the Gold Coast. The main Danish ports of destination in the Western hemisphere were St. Thomas, St. John and St. Croix. To quote Donnan, *"Most of these cargoes came from Guineau, though Negroes from Calabar, Loango, Angola, and even Madagascar appear in the list."*

Goldbery made this comment about French trafficking on the Isle of Gambra in 1786:

"In 1781 Hannibal died, and left his establishment and commerce to M. Ancel, who, in 1785, and in the first months of 1786, had, as appeared by his journals, purchased one hundred and forty-two slaves, at the average price of two hundred francs per head . . . This commerce was not quite so active during the war for the independence of America, but at the peace of 1783, it was resumed with insatiable ardor. Whole chains of captives arrived from all parts, at the market for the trade, and we were astonished to learn, that many of these caravans of slaves did not arrive at Galam in the Senegal, at Barraconda, in the Gambra, and at the factories of the rivers of Sherbroo, Gabon, Volte, Benin, and the river Zaira, before they had performed marches of sixty, seventy, and eighty days; and by calculating the extent of these routes, it was evident that they must have come from the most central regions of Africa. We may therefore be convinced, that the interior of this Continent is not so desert a space as has long been imagined.

THE RACIALIZATION OF SLAVERY

[FYI: modern researchers from Chancellor Williams to James Owen have divulged the fact that the topography of the Sahara was once lush and tropical.] According to the results of the slave-trade on the coasts of Africa, from the year 1765 to 1785, the exportation of blacks, bought by the European factories along the coasts, was estimated at sixty thousand captives per annum, and in 1786 and 1787 the number exceeded seventy thousand head in each year . . . In short, we saw the number of exported blacks increase, and by a report made on the slave trade in 1790, by the Privy Council of the king of England, and afterwards by the House of Commons, we learned that during the years 1787, 1788, and 1789, the Europeans had exported from Africa nearly eighty thousand negroes per annum . . ."

When it comes to the English trade, in 1672, trafficker documents sent to the Royal African Company stated the following:
"Next begins the North coast of Guinea. On James Island in the River Gambia the companies have a fort where are kept 70

men, and a factory whence elephants' teeth, bees-wax, and cowhides are exported in very considerable quantities; the river is very large and runs up much higher than any discovery has been made, and the gold is supposed to come most from places at its head; in this river they have small factories at Rio Noones, Rispongo, and Calsamanca, and trade by sloops to Rio Grande and Catchao, [region southeast of the Gambia River] for those commodities and negroes . . . At Cape Trespontes begins the trade for gold, and on that coast they have factories, not laid down in the maps, at Ashinee, Abinee, Dixiscove, Anashan, Anto, Succondee, Anamaboo, Wyamba and Aga; Cormentine was taken from them in the first Dutch war, when Mr. Selwyn was agent, and at the same time they took Cabo-Corso Castle from the Dutch, which is now their chief port and place of trade, with 100 English, besides slaves, and the residence of their Agent-General, who furnishes thence all their under-factories with goods, and receives from them gold, elephants' teeth and slaves. Near Cabo-Corso is the great Dutch castle called the

The Racialization of Slavery

Mina; and more leewardly [nautical term for the opposite direction of windward] the company have another factory at Acra for gold. Their next factory is at Ardra for slaves only, which are there very plentiful; next follows Benin with a factory where they procure great quantities of cotton cloths to sell at Cabo-Corso and on the Gold Coast; then more leewardly lies the Bite, whither many ships are sent to trade at New and Old Calabar for slaves and teeth, which are there to be had in great plenty, and also in the rivers Cameroons and Gaboons . . . A trade for Angola is begun, and they have ordered a factory to settle near the Portugals' chief city at Sunis, whence it is hoped great quantities of slaves and copper may be got . . . The slaves are sent to all his Majesty's American Plantations which cannot subsist without them . . ."

In the 17th century records of John Barbot we also find this interesting account about the trade:
"The English have also a lodge at Offra, but the Dutch having the preeminence in commerce, as being the first intruders at

Ardra, they carry a great sway over the English; and one year with another export above three thousand slaves. The Portuguese, in the beginning of this century, had a considerable trade there, but were supplanted by the Hollanders . . . Several of those Blacks act therein as factors, or brokers, either for their own countrymen, or for the Europeans; who are often obliged to trust them with their goods, to attend the upper markets, and purchase slaves for them: for all that vast number of slaves, which the Calabar Blacks sell to all European nations, but more especially to the Hollanders, who have there the greatest trade, are not their prisoners at war, the greatest part being bought by those people of their inland neighbours, and they also buy them of other nations yet more remote from them . . . Of all European trading nations that frequent this river, and the adjacent parts, the Dutch have the greatest share in the trade; the English next, and after them the Portuguese, from Brasil, St. Thome and Prince's islands; and all altogether export thence a great number of slaves yearly to America, besides a considerable quantity

THE RACIALIZATION OF SLAVERY

of good elephant's teeth, and abundance of provisions . . ."[7]

Regions Instrumental in the Transatlantic Trade

---

[7] Donnan, E., <u>Documents Illustrative of the History of the Slave Trade to America</u> Vol. I, p. 7, 192 - 193, 298 - 300, 458, Vol. II, pp. xiv - xvi, 566 - 567 & Thomas, H., <u>The Slave Trade</u> p. 388

<u>It is clear that the uncompensated labor of captive and brutalized Africans produced untold riches for the wealthy of Western Europe and the Americas</u>. By the by, it is said that the Spanish desired, *"the blackest sort with short curled hair,"* of the Madagascans. Finally, one cannot help but note the use of the term <u>factory</u> (*as in a place were resources are processed or refined*) in relation to the locales where human beings were held in captivity, stripped of their humanity, and sold: <u>African life reduced to a commodity</u> . . .

The Transatlantic Trafficking Of Humans

To illustrate the proliferation of the West's trade in human cargo, Curtin makes the astonishing disclosure, *"more Africans than Europeans arrived in the Americas between, say, 1492 and 1770."*[8] He continues:

> *"It is now possible to look at the long-term movement of the Atlantic slave trade over a period of more than four centuries . . . Together, these data make it abundantly clear that the eighteenth century was a kind of plateau in the history of the trade—the period when the trade reached its height, but also a period of slackening growth and beginning decline. The period 1741-1810 marks the summit of the plateau, when the long-term annual average rates of delivery hung just above*

---
[8] Curtin, P., <u>The Atlantic Slave Trade: A Census</u> p. 87, 158 & Rosen, R., <u>A Short History of Charleston</u> p. 73
He also explains that from 1701 to 1775, the majority of the Africans who were enslaved in the Southern States arrived at Chesapeake Bay or Charleston South Carolina. Charleston actually came to be seen as the "Capital of Southern Slavery."

60,000 a year. The edge of the plateau was reached, however, just after the Peace of Utrecht [Netherlands] in 1713, when the annual deliveries began regularly to exceed 40,000 a year, and the permanent drop below 40,000 a year did not come again until after the 1840's. <u>Thus about 60 per cent of all slaves delivered to the New World were transported during the century 1721-1820. Eighty per cent of the total were landed during the century and a half, 1701-1850.</u>"[9]

Philip Curtin has also labored to produce a rough tabulation (in percentage points) of the African regions of departure for the people brought to North America: 13.3 from Senegambia; 5.5 from Sierra Leone; 11.4 from Windward Coast (Iberia-Ivory Coast); 15.9 from

---

[9] Curtin, P., <u>The Atlantic Slave Trade: A Census</u> p. 265

Gold Coast; 4.3 from Benin; 23.3 from Biafra (Southeastern Nigeria); 24.5 from Angola; 1.6 from Mozambique and Madagascar; and 0.2 unknown. Once more, so as not to mislead anyone, the said percentages are estimates and cannot be said to factually represent the ancestral make-up of Blacks in North America today.[10]

---

[10] Curtin, P., The Atlantic Slave Trade: A Census pp. 25 - 26, 75 - 79, 157 & Donnan, E., Documents Illustrative of the History of the Slave Trade to America Vol. I, p. v

One other aspect of the triangular trade that must not escape our notice is nations did not always retain the people they took from Africa. Hence, fairly close ancestral ties could exist between diverse populations of Blacks in the Western hemisphere today—despite living in different countries and/or even speaking different languages. For instance, Curtin tells us that British slavers routinely transported more Africans than could be sold in their colonies. Consequently, Spanish and French slavers were permitted to come to the British colonies and buy Africans whom they then took to South America, Mexico and the Caribbean. A common scenario could well have been for two related children to be taken from the Kongo by the British and brought to America. Later, a Frenchman could buy and take one of them to Martinique—while his captive sister or cousin remained in North America. This is one of the reasons that Donnan would assert: *"The traffic to the thirteen colonies, to the West Indies, and to Spanish America was so closely interwoven that to a certain extent it seemed necessary to treat it as a whole."*

The Racialization of Slavery

African captive being sold in Easton Maryland c. 1850

Serious efforts to halt the transatlantic trade by the culprit nations were not undertaken until the end of the 18th century. In 1792, Denmark would become the first nation to cease their involvement in the trade. The British stopped trafficking in 1807. A year later, the American Congress placed a prohibition against the <u>importation</u> of African slaves. The French did not abolish slavery until 1848; the Dutch, 1863; the U.S., in 1865; and the Portuguese and Spanish not until 1888. Atop this, Sir Henry Stanley would report that the Arab slave trade was still active in Africa as late as the 1890s.[11]

---

[11] Slavery, <u>The American Peoples Encyclopedia</u> Vol. XVII, pp. 764 - 765 & Slavery, <u>The World Book Encyclopedia</u> Vol. XV, p. 7498 & Slavery, <u>Encyclopedia Americana</u> Vol. XXV, p. 24 & Donnan, E., <u>Documents Illustrative of the History of the Slave Trade to America</u> & Keith, A., <u>The Berlin Congo and the Berlin Act</u> pp. 92 - 100 & (Video), <u>Tony Brown's Journal: A First Hand View of Slavery in Africa</u> & Rowntree, J., <u>The Imperial Drug Trade</u> & (Video), Booknotes: Interview with Robert Skidelsky: <u>John Maynard Keynes</u> Vol. III C-Span 4/02
<u>Unbelievably, Samuel Cotton makes the disclosure that Arabs still hold untold numbers of Africans in slavery.</u> In passing, while the English are to be applauded for their efforts to stop

THE RACIALIZATION OF SLAVERY

Chinese officials destroying British opium c.1750 CE

the trade, it must be said that in this same period British merchants were making tremendous profits from opium trading, which would be responsible for producing millions of addicts (drug slaves) in Asia. <u>*Isn't it interesting that drugs that are said to make the masses high—render them so low*</u>? Rowntree observed that both, Europe's India grown opium and Christian missionaries would arrive in China at the exact same time. Further here, <u>Queen Victoria and her government are known to have consciously sanctioned the opium trade</u>. In light of this, it's hardly surprising that China's Prince Kung should admonish the English: *"Take away your opium and your missionaries, and you will be welcome . . ."* Yet, through the enactment of many unsavory political measures (culminating in the Opium Wars) the English would gain control of the Chinese island of Hong Kong. With this, they maintained a profitable Asian revenue stream through the peddling of opium in China for more than a century. Ironic that even with the opium trade and all of their 19th century colonies, the British Empire would face economic collapse twice: defaulting on its financial debt after WWI and needing to be bailed out of its financial obligations by the United States during WWII through Roosevelt's Lend-Lease legislation. Photo appears courtesy of Wikimedia.

Cultural Ties & Distant Lineages

THE RACIALIZATION OF SLAVERY

Many individuals of African heritage in the West have wondered, *From which African people did I descend*? This is understandable for so much as—*a man without knowledge of himself, is like a tree with no roots.* Of course, for many, this question will never be answered. Yet, because of the efforts of scores of diligent scholars, some interesting overall determinations can be made.[1]

---

[1] Rosen, R., A Short History of Charleston & Milele, N., The Journey of the Songhai People p. 214 & Jackson, P., When Roots Die & Stuckey, S., Slave Culture p. 12
Cultural anthropologists have found evidence of many connections between Africans of the Eastern and Western hemispheres. Jackson notes linguistic similarities between Blacks in the Sea Islands and the Ewe, Fante, Efik, Ibebio, Yoruba, Twi, Kongo and Mandinka of West Africa. Also, Stuckey writes: "*In Bakongo burial ceremonies . . . bodies were sometimes laid out in state in an open yard 'on a textile-decorated bier,' as bare-chested mourners danced to the rhythms of drums 'in a broken counter-clockwise circle . . .' Wherever in Africa the counterclockwise dance ceremony was performed—it is called the ring shout in North America—the dancing and singing were directed to the ancestors and gods . . . The ring in which Africans danced and sang is the key to understanding the means by which they achieved oneness in America. Knowledge of the ancestral dance in Dahomey contributes to that understanding and helps explain aspects of the shout in North America . . . For instance, the solo ring*

DISTANT LINEAGES & CULTURAL TIES

In broad terms, investigating the transatlantic trade leaves little doubt that a large number of the Africans taken into captivity were not full citizens of a west coast kingdom. While slavers were to randomly kidnap some coastal Africans, it is incorrect to depict this as the way that the majority of Africans were obtained.

Truth be told, although ships were to depart from the west coast, many of the Africans who made the transatlantic crossing were actually from the continent's interior regions; however, happenstance either rendered them subject to a coastal ruler, or the terrible act of manstealing (kidnapping).[2] According to Alton Hornsby:

---

shouts noted by Lydia Parrish in Virginia and North Carolina are in the ring dances of Dahomey." Such cultural associations are informative and can be very useful.
[2] Donnan, E., Documents Illustrative of the History of the Slave Trade to America Vol. II, pp. 633 - 634 & Klein, H., The Middle Passage p. 242
Large numbers of the Africans sold to the Europeans were captives of war, or people who were purchased inland by African slavers, which generally afforded them few, to no,

THE RACIALIZATION OF SLAVERY

"The ancestors of most black Americans came from the area of Africa known as Western Sudan. This area extended from the Atlantic Ocean in the west to Lake Chad in the east, and from the Sahara desert in the north to the Gulf of Guinea [and beyond] in the south."[3]

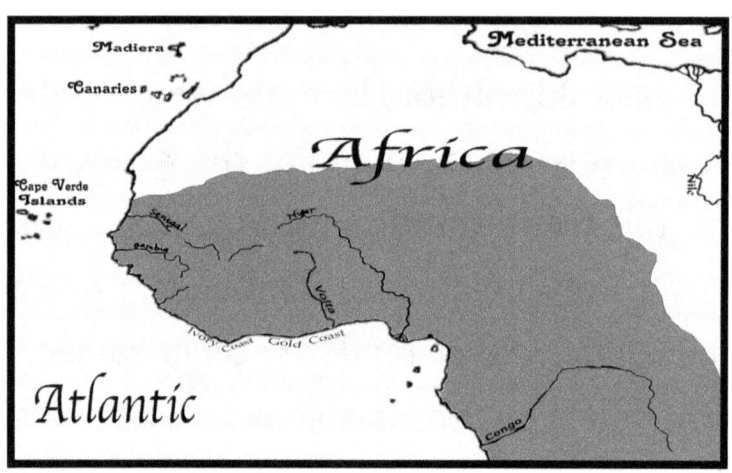

Dark area represents the regions on the continent where most Africans were seized

rights or protections on the sea coast. On the other hand, if a citizen of a coastal kingdom was cast into slavery (e.g., for a criminal offense or due to a failure to pay a big debt) friends or family members (through a ransom of goods or other Africans) could secure that person's freedom from traffickers.
[3] Hornsby, A., Chronology of African American History p. xiii & Davis, E., The First Sex p. 124
Davis comments, *"Modern Sudan, in ancient times was a colony of Egypt populated by Egyptians."*

Distant Lineages & Cultural Ties

The peoples of Africa have long maintained that the peoples of West Africa migrated there from the eastern and northern parts of the continent. As a matter of fact, in Alex Haley's Roots, it is explained that although Kunta Kinte was taken from Gambia, his grandfather, Kairaba Kunta Kinte, was a Moslem who had migrated south into that region from Mauritania.[4]

Interestingly, the noted Egyptologist Wallis Budge wrote: *"The earliest kings of Egypt were exact counterparts of the kings of Dahomey, Congo-land, Dar fur, Unyoro, Uganda, &c., described in the Travels of Skertchley, Burton, Stanley, Speke, Baker, Johnson, and others, and there is little doubt that they were of Sudani [Nile Valley] origin."*[5] It also warrants mention here that many words in the ancient Egyptian

---

[4] Haley, A., Roots p. 13
[5] Budge, E.A., A Short History of the Egyptian People pp. 192 - 193

language, and that of the peoples of Western Africa, are virtually identical.

Researchers have made a plethora of findings that establish cultural connections between the peoples of Western Africa and the Nile Valley. For instance, archeologists have discovered Egyptian-styled artifacts in the region of Timbuktu that date to Pre-Dynastic times (c.3500 BCE). Further, astronomers tell us that just like the Egyptians of old, the Dogon of Mali do not merely pay tribute to Sirius—but plot the 50-year elliptical orbit of Sirius-B as well! *In passing, Sirius-B just happens to be invisible to the human eye from the earth.*

The celebrated Ra Un Nefer Amen makes many spiritual associations between ancient Egypt and the later societies of Western Africa. We even find corroborating evidence in this declaration by Keating:

" The influence of Meroe has lingered on . . . All over West and Central Africa strange similarities of form have appeared . . . Nubian speaking peoples, living today in Western and Southwestern Sudan, still preserve the ancient name of Kush . . . remains of cities have been reported from remote corners of the Kordofan and Darfur provinces which, on examination, may prove to be of Meroitic origin; two bronze lamps from a grave in Ghana strongly resemble lamps found in burial mounds of the fifth century in Nubia; to this day in Benin City, Nigeria, bronze objects are being made which recall strongly some of the bronzes made in Meroe and Egypt to commemorate the god Amun."[6]

---

[6] Diop, C.A., The African Origin of Civilization: Myth Or Reality pp. 179 - 200 & Van Sertima, I., Blacks in Science: Ancient and Modern pp. 27 - 44 & Timbuktu, Collier's Encyclopedia Vol. 22, p. 317 & Bauval, R., & Gilbert, A.,

The Racialization of Slavery

The principal explanation for migration is a tremendous drought and famine in East-central Africa. Yet, whether for drought, exploration, war, or some other reason—there is little doubt that large migrations occurred which brought many Northeastern Africans into the continent's Central and Western regions by the 15th century.[7]

Having shared all of this, <u>the significance of these findings is that the immediate ancestors of many of the people of African heritage in the West today were, in fact, descendants of the ancient inhabitants of Northern and Eastern Africa</u>. In deference here to Davidson:

<u>The Orion Mystery</u> pp. 96 - 97 & Berlitz, C., <u>Atlantis: The Eight Continent</u> pp. 139 - 140 & De Lubicz, R., <u>Sacred Science: The King of Pharaonic Theocracy</u> pp. 173 - 175, 289 & Keating, R., <u>Nubian Twilight</u> pp. 72 - 73
[7] (Video), <u>The Mystery of the Sphinx</u> Discovery 1996 & (Video), <u>The Nature of Things Radar: Images From Space</u> C.B.C. 1987 & Williams, C., <u>The Destruction of Black Civilization</u> pp. 183 - 187 & Sjoo, M., & Mor, B., <u>The Great Cosmic Mother</u> p. 21 & (Video), <u>Chronicle: Egypt</u> 1990 & Burn, A., & Selincourt, A., <u>Herodotus: The Histories</u> p. 133

DISTANT LINEAGES & CULTURAL TIES

"The point is that they 'marched' most precisely from the middle Nile to the middle Niger: along a trans-African trade route . . . which migrating peoples undoubtedly used from times that are exceedingly remote . . . Even today thousands of Nigerian pilgrims follow it to the Red Sea every year, and other thousands follow it back again; and two thousand years ago and more the climate and vegetation would have treated trans-African travelers in a gentler way than they do now . . . There is practically no well-known people in West Africa without its legend of an eastern or northern origin in the remote past . . . Increasingly one sees that the 'stagnant centuries' of tribal Africa have only been a figment of the imagination."[8]

---

[8] Davidson, B., The Lost Cities of Africa pp. 59 - 64 & Diop, C.A., The African Origin of Civilization: Myth Or Reality pp.

The Racialization of Slavery

In conclusion, many Western writers reflexively reject the idea that Africans in the Western hemisphere are in any way related to the ancient peoples of Eastern Africa. It is rather amusing to watch the mental gymnastics that some have

---

184 - 187 & Davidson, B., History of West Africa to the Nineteenth Century pp. 118 - 119 & Davis, E., The First Sex p. 124 & Worthy, R., About Black Hair
Davidson continues: "*Biobaku has felt able to suggest that the founders of Yoruba civilization in southern Nigeria reached their country between the seventh and tenth centuries A.D., coming originally from the middle Nile . . . the ram, symbol of Amun, became one of the great divine symbols of Kush. Even to this day you may find many granite rams at Meroe and Naga . . . Many West African peoples celebrated its divinity. The Mandinka of the Western Sudan consider that the god of storm and thunder takes earthly shape as a ram. The Yoruba national god, Shango, appears with a ram's mask and is equally the god of storm and thunder. The Baoule of the Ivory Coast represent Niannie,, the personalized sky, with the mask of a ram; and the god of lightning is also a ram for the Fon people of Dahomey . . . Wainwright has shown how priestly breastplates, from Yorubaland in Southern Nigeria of the medieval period, recall similar models dedicated to Amun in dynastic Egypt . . .*" The photo (page 161) is of two royal singers of Amun-Ra during ancient Egypt's 20th Dynasty. The artifact is housed in the British Museum in London England. Incidentally, this man is not wearing a wig. The ancient Egyptians commonly wore their hair in the natural style commonly known today as, "dread-locks."

undergone to *negate* this reality. But it strains all credulity to acknowledge, and at times even celebrate, the ancient Egyptian presence in the Mediterranean, Europe, and Asia—*but suddenly become unable to fathom how these same people could possibly negotiate far shorter distances, on their native continent, over many centuries, when having much more at stake!*

Egyptian Noble Couple c. 1200 BCE

Treatment Of The Enslaved Through The Ages

TREATMENT OF THE ENSLAVED

It is wrong to assert that the inhuman treatment inflicted upon Blacks by Whites during slavery in the Americas need not be condemned since many Old World societies had slaves. Of course, it is true that men and women of all races have been held in subjugation throughout history. Furthermore, it is clear that martial force and some violence has played a role in that enslavement.

However, one would be gravely mistaken were they to conclude the following: (1), centuries of kidnapping; (2), name changing; (3), denial of one's native language; (4), branding of the flesh; (5), deliberate undernourishment; (6), no legal protection of person; (7), proscriptions against education; (8), proscriptions against marriage; (9), random rape and murder; and (10), that subjugation set in virtual perpetuity (based on physical appearance) were universal staples of Old World slavery!

The Racialization of Slavery

Don't get me wrong, I am not declaring ancient slavery to have been a weekend fish fry; yet, it is clear that having martial authority over someone was not considered a license to try to strip them of their humanity: *the ancients understood that a willingness to murder the powerless is no measure of manhood.* Truth be told, civilizations from Egypt, to Arabia, to Mesopotamia, to Rome, to Andalusia—did not merely frown on brutality towards slaves—they enacted laws to protect them from rank cruelty.

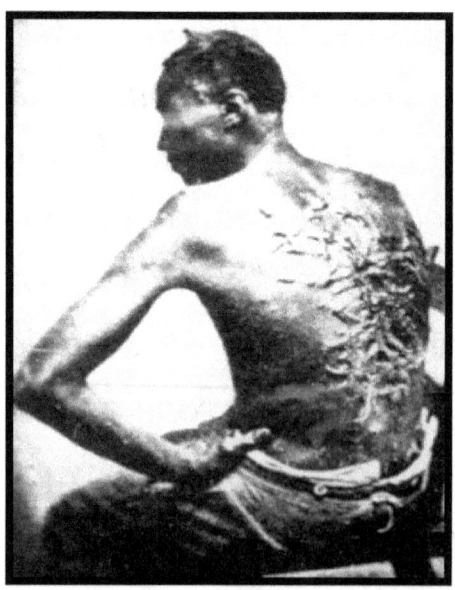

Evidence of the brutality of American slavery

Even more, to intergenerationally enslave people because of their biology (*in this case having activated melanin*) was completely unheard of! But in that we have already discussed the fact that racially based slavery was a late practice, I want to briefly touch upon the relative benevolence of Old World slavery as compared to that of the later West:

> In the ancient Egyptian civilization, all children were born free. Thus, the child of a slave mother was free to experience the same life as other free children in Egypt. David asserts, "*It was not unusual for a slave to reach a position of trust.*" And Wilson writes, "*Egypt had no rigid caste system, in which nobles, artisans, peasants and slaves were restrained to a single class for generation upon generation . . .*" These disclosures do not represent aberrations. Across Africa it was not uncommon for members of a defeated society (commonly the slave class) to participate in many facets of dominant society life—from culture, to business, to

THE RACIALIZATION OF SLAVERY

government and even the military in some instances. To further demonstrate the magnanimity of African slavery, <u>scholars explain that in many cases the slave class performed the exact tasks, with similar recompense, as free people of the society</u>. Though maintaining their tribal identity and seen as people outside of the dominant tribe—loyalty, dedication, and/or simple good fortune, could lead to prosperity and even freedom for the enslaved.

Code of Hammurabi c. 1750 BCE

Moving east, Saggs reveals the fact that the Code of Hammurabi called for fixed time limits of enslavement. The length was set according to the offense; for example, if a person could not repay a debt, they could be held in subjugation for three years.

About the practice of Hebrew slavery it is explained:
"The Hebrew slave was not forced to serve for more than six years . . . There were a number of ways by which a Hebrew could fall into bondage, the most frequent being his inability to pay a debt . . . If poverty was the reason for servitude the slave had to be treated not as a bondsman but as a hired servant, and was to serve until the year of the jubilee . . . If a Hebrew was sold to a stranger his brethren had to redeem him . . . and the same applied to Hebrew prisoners of war . . . The servitude of a Hebrew slave did not bring about any change in his social and personal status: after completing his term he was free to go to his own house . . . Some slaves reached positions of eminence, examples being Eliezer, Abraham's slave . . . In some cases the master's daughter could be given to a

THE RACIALIZATION OF SLAVERY

slave . . . A slave was allowed to acquire possessions of his own, including other slaves . . . and use the income in order to redeem himself . . . According to Deuteronomy (23:15) a fugitive slave was not to be handed back to his owner . . ."

Some in the West have attempted to use the Bible to justify the inhumanity of Western slavery. But <u>Deuteronomy</u> 15:14-15 of the Old Testament instructs the Hebrews that it was a duty of all masters to generously provide for their slaves: *"Thou shalt furnish him liberally out of thy flock, and out of thy floor, and out of thy winepress: of that wherewith the Lord thy God hath blessed thee, thou shalt give unto him."*

Moreover, contemporary Bible scholars state:
"The NT [New Testament] urges the acceptance of the slave as brother . . . Slaves are not to be abused (Eph 6:9), but to be treated with equality and fairness (Col 4:1). <u>Revelation</u> 18:13 decries the inhumanity of the slave trade and <u>I Timothy</u> 1:9-10 classifies slave-kidnapers

among the 'unholy and profane.'" Indeed, Exodus 21:16 and Deuteronomy 24:7 even call for the death penalty for kidnappers of free people that were sold into slavery.

Blake and Watson maintain that the later Romans also had strong laws prohibiting cruelty and the murdering of slaves.

Lastly here, Lane-Poole would say the following about Moorish slavery:
"Slavery is a very mild and humane institution in the hands of a good Mohammedan . . . 'God . . . hath ordained that your brothers should be your slaves: therefore him whom God hath to be the slave of his brother, his brother must give him the food which he eateth himself, and of the clothes wherewith he clotheth himself, and not order him to do anything beyond his power . . . A man who ill-treats a slave will not enter into Paradise.'"
He continued:
"Instead of being hopelessly condemned to servitude for all their lives . . . they had only to go to the nearest Mohammedan of repute, and repeat the formula of belief, 'There is no god but God, and Mohammed

THE RACIALIZATION OF SLAVERY

is his Prophet,' and they became immediately free."[1]

Hence, it is clear that the blue print for the depraved behavior of the slavers of the New

---

[1] Murphy, E., Diodorus on Egypt p. 104 & David, R., The Egyptian Kingdoms p. 108 & Wilson, J., Culture of Ancient Egypt p. 75 & Saggs, H., Civilization before Greece and Rome pp. 157 - 158 & Hebrews, Illustrated Dictionary & Concordance of the Bible pp. 944 - 945 & Duckat, W., Beggar to King pp. 231 - 234 & Blake, W., History of Slavery and the Slave Trade pp. 57 - 58 & Watson, A., The Law of the Ancient Romans & Lane-Poole, S., The Moors in Spain pp. 48 - 49 & Van Sertima, I., The Golden Age of the Moor pp. 198 - 199 & Rosen, R., A Short History of Carolina pp. 67 - 69 & Elkins, S., Slavery pp. 53 - 54, 59, 130 - 131 & Fogel, R., Time on the Cross p. 141 & Altman, S., The Encyclopedia of African-American Heritage p. 30

Though previously touching upon the **Slave Codes** (see page 101), I should add that the prohibition against African marriages made it easier for slavers to split couples: <u>selling one individual of the union to another slaveholder without legal ramifications or any regard for the Black family</u>. The practice also helped to negate the Black male's standing as father, or head, of the family unit. The design was for Black youth to be taught that it was only the White plantation owner who was smart enough to be a father. Of course, once Black males became older and seen as no threat to the plantation owner—children could then call them <u>uncle</u> so-and-so. Obviously, this all was only marginally effective: women loving their mates, and Black males occupying practically all of the managerial positions open to them. However, <u>Black marriages and families were not legally recognized in the South until after the Civil War in 1866</u>.

World was based much more in the Western European mind than the Bible or societies of the Old World. You needn't take my word for this; the whole world knows this to be so! In 1799, General Eaton, Consul of the United States at Tunisia, declared: *"Truth and justice demand from me the confession, that the Christian slaves amongst the barbarians of Africa are treated with more humanity than the African slaves among the Christians of civilized America..."*[2]

Atlanta Georgia store where captives were sold

---

[2] Blake, W., History of Slavery and the Slave Trade p. 79
Photo taken in 1864 of slave business on Whitehall Street. It appears courtesy of the Library of Congress.

The Racialization of Slavery

In actual point fact, the barbarism of Western slavery was so far afield from the historical norms that many Whites felt compelled to condemn it well before the Civil War. For example, in 1836 Theodore Weld wrote: *"Slavery in itself is cruelty—atrocious cruelty; that in the system cruelty is the rule, not the exception; that those who hold human beings as property will inflict upon them greater cruelties than they do upon their brutes, I know from years of personal observation in the midst of southern slavery . . ."*[3]

Even more stirring, Lord Palmerston would address the British House of Commons thusly: *"I will venture to say that if all the crimes which the human race has committed from the Creation down to the present day were added together in one vast aggregate, they would*

---

[3] Aptheker, H., <u>American Negro Slave Revolts</u> pp. 132 - 133

scarcely equal, I am sure they could not exceed, the amount of guilt which had been incurred by mankind in connection with this diabolical slave trade."[4]

**Slave hut on Boone's plantation - South Carolina
Open room about 30 by 15 feet (said for up to ten people)**

Finally here, *while historians know such a stance to be absurd*, insomuch as there are those who feel that the inhumanity heaped upon the African should have no moral consequence since

---

[4] Halasz, N., The Rattling Chains p. 191

THE RACIALIZATION OF SLAVERY

they were nothing but <u>ignorant savages</u>—I shall close with a comment by the famed European explorer David Livingstone. After witnessing the wretched undertakings of slave traffickers against a countless number of peaceful, and often defenseless, Africans—the 19th century Scotsman would be moved to remark:

> *"I have no prejudice against their colour; indeed, any one who lives long among them forgets that they are Black and feels that they are just fellow-men . . . If a comparison were instituted, and Manyuema [people of Tanzania] taken at random, placed opposite say the members of the Anthropological Society of London, clad like them in kilts of grass cloth, I should like to take my place among the Manyuema, on the principle of preferring the company of my betters . . ."*[5]

---

[5] Jeal, T., <u>Livingstone</u> pp. 101 - 106, 153 - 154, 345 - 346

African Freedom Fighters

The Racialization of Slavery

In 1795, C.B. Wadstrom would divulge the following in a report by the directors of the Sierra Leone Company about the transatlantic slave trade:

> "*They are chiefly brought down through a chain of factories, but not through the company's ground, and a great many are children. The kings and chiefs trade in slaves; but the principal traders are the French and English factors. It is customary to credit the black factors who either travel themselves, or deal with other factors still farther up [inland], with European goods (chiefly gunpowder and spirits) and, if they fail in bringing the stipulated slaves, they are made slaves themselves; or, if they do not return in a certain time, any one of their families are taken . . . kidnapping prevails at Sierra Leona, the directors have received undeniable proofs; and, if they had not,*

several circumstances clearly imply that the practice is not uncommon. The inhabitants, to a great distance up the country, all go armed with guns and large knives. The very women are armed with knives. When King Naimbanna's son has gone up to Scaffus, he dared not go to rest, unless in a secure place, lest he should be surprised in his sleep. The people in the little towns on the river, leave the wood growing close to the houses, for refuge, in case of attack, as they told Mr. Falconbridge, who has seen the ruins of two towns, which, among others, were broken up by Cleveland, a great mulatto slave-trader who was educated at Liverpool..."[1]

---

[1] Donnan, E., Documents Illustrative of the History of the Slave Trade to America Vol. II, pp. 618 - 619 & Halasz, N., The Rattling Chains p. 119

THE RACIALIZATION OF SLAVERY

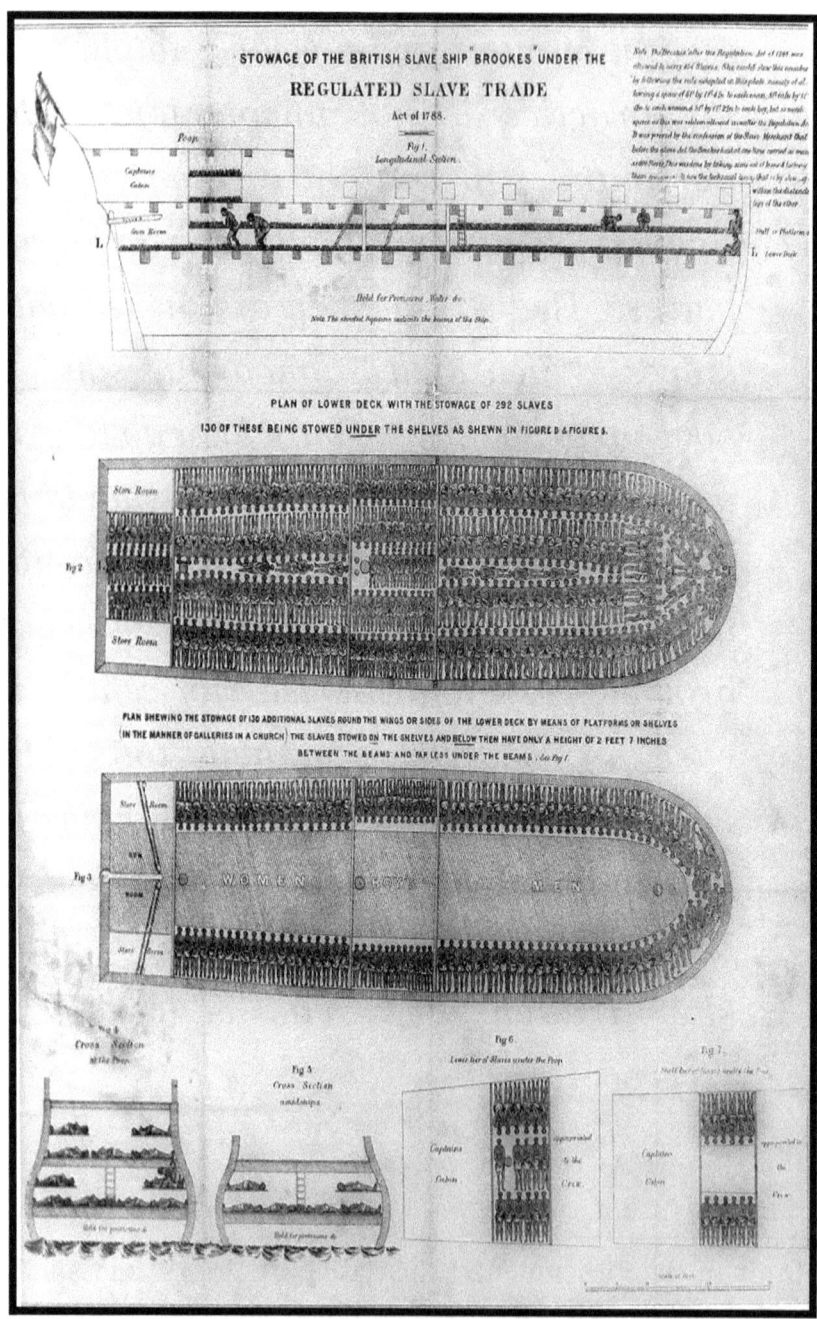

Diagram of British ship loaded with 454 people in 1788

There isn't any doubt that White slavers would never have been able to secure the millions of Africans that they transported across the Atlantic had it not been for the willing participation of many African rulers and facilitators. Thomas explains that the vast majority of Africans were sold to Europeans by the continent's kings, nobles, or their agents. John Barbot wrote:

> *"Tis usual for Europeans, to give the king the value of fifty slaves in goods, for his permission to trade, and customs for each ship; and to the king's son, the value of two slaves, for the privilege of watering; and of four slaves for wooding, in case it be wanted . . . The factor or supercargo having finished his sale, is to present the king again with two muskets, twenty five pounds of powder, and the value of nine slaves in other goods, as an acknowledgement to that prince for his*

favour in granting him the permission to trade in his dominions . . ."[2]

The Triangular Trade
(see page 131)

While this complicity is undeniable, it must also be stated that many African rulers could not stomach slave trafficking in their lands. In actual point of fact, hundreds of martial

---
[2] Thomas, H., The Slave Trade pp. 388 - 389 & Donnan, E., Documents Illustrative of the History of the Slave Trade to America Vol. I, pp. 296 - 297
This was a 1682 eyewitness account of the trade in Ardra Guinea. Historical illustration (page 178) appears courtesy of the Library of Congress. Map of Triangular Trade courtesy of Creative Commons SA-2.5

engagements to free captives from slavers did not only take place in the Caribbean and the Americas—but on the African continent as well! Thus, contrary to the oft presented Western depictions of the unconscious African ruler and happy-go-lucky crying slave—<u>countless numbers of Africans undertook whatever action they could to overthrow their captivity and the trade: Africans destroyed ships; they killed slavers; they carried out labor strikes; they mutilated their bodies; and, even committed suicide before allowing themselves to be enslaved</u>.

For example, Western chroniclers describe the daring revolt of Yanga as one of the most successful rebellions in Mexican history:

> *"In 1609 the viceroy sent an army of six hundred men against Yanga, whose camp had eighty men and some women and children. The viceroy's soldiers were given some lessons in guerrilla maneuvers by*

Yanga, and [after many years] when the skirmishing finally ended in a standoff, the government agreed to treat [terms] with the Black rebel . . . Not long afterward an independent black town, San Lorenzo de los Negros, was founded near Cordoba."

Elsewhere, after decades of fighting, 1500 Black Maroons of Jamaica forced the British into a peace treaty: *terms including safe passage back to Sierra Leone.* Zumbi of Palmares Brazil was a dynamic Black fighter who led some 20,000 followers in Brazil during the 17th century. Miguel Guacamaya, Juan Andresote and Jose Chirinos were great warriors in Venezuela. But, of course, no hero of the age was more heralded than Toussaint L'Ouverture—who in 1797 defeated the French and British to found Haiti.[3]

---

[3] Okihiro, G., In Resistance: Studies in African, Caribbean and Afro-American History & Meyer, M., & Sherman, W., The

African Freedom Fighters

French depiction of Toussaint L'Ouverture in 1802

Course of Mexican History pp. 216 - 217 & Campbell, M., The Maroons of Jamaica 1655 - 1796 & Stewart, W., & Peterson, H., Builders of Latin America & Rout, L., The African Experience in Spanish America & Beard, J., The Life of Toussaint L'Ouverture & Aptheker, H., American Negro Slave Revolts pp. 142 - 143 & Halasz, N., The Rattling Chains & James, C., A History of Negro Revolt

In a widely reported case in 1807, two shiploads of newly transported African captives chose to starve themselves to death, rather than submit to slavery in South Carolina.

THE RACIALIZATION OF SLAVERY

In the words of Herbert Aptheker: "*Individual attempts at assassination or property damage by gun, knife, club, axe, poison, or fire were so numerous that undertaking an enumeration of all would be a well-nigh impossible task.*"[4] Though concurring, permit me to share a few contemporaneous reports of the martial engagements of Africans, *in the East and West*, to stop the kidnapping and enslavement of their sistren and brethren:

> Correspondence from Captain Bernard Ladman to the Royal African Company in 1701 stated:
> "*Accordingly on the 27th of Dec. Capt. Daniel Lowis, of the Dolphin sloop belonging to London, being at anchor off of Drewin to trade, great numbers of Negroes came to trade; and surprised them all, took all that was in the vessel and ran her ashore, where she staved in pieces. The mate and boatswain escaped*

---
[4] Aptheker, H., American Negro Slave Revolts p. 143

in the boat, but the commander and the rest of his men, they drove up into the country . . ."

The Newport Customs House provides this 18th century narrative of an African uprising aboard ship during a transatlantic crossing:

"The 'Little George' had sailed from the Guinea coast for Rhode Island in June of 1730, with 96 slaves aboard, of whom 35 were men. The latter somehow 'got off their iron' on June 6 at dawn. Captain George Scott, the mates, and a cabin boy barricaded themselves in the cabin, while the slaves tried to turn the ship towards shore. After four days the whites noticed that the ship had returned to the same point where it had lain when the slaves had taken over. While they navigated, the slaves 'were continually heaving down Billets of Wood, and Water into the cabin, with the intention to Disable us and spoil our small arms,' Captain Scott reported. However, the captain and crew came up with a plan of their own. They bored holes through the bottom of the vessel and let in about three feet of water. Then the

THE RACIALIZATION OF SLAVERY

captain called to the slaves and stated that he would sink the ship with all of them. The frightened slaves were cajoled into promising to land the ship and leave it intact. The captain shouted navigating directions through the closed cabin door and when the ship was beached the slaves hastened onto shore and disappeared. Natives drawn by the spectacle of the beached ship then thronged the shore, excited by the prospect of seizing the ship and its treasures. They fired on the vessel and were preparing to climb aboard when an English ship approached and saved the embattled crew members, who had survived their nine-day imprisonment in the cabin by eating stored rice and water."

A 1739 Charleston news article entitled, <u>Slaves revolt; many die</u>, reported:
"A series of slave revolts has jolted South Carolina, leaving dozens dead at Charleston, Stono River and Berkeley County. Local people charge that the rebellions were incited by Spanish missionaries who created among the slaves a false expectation of delivery from bondage. The Charleston insurrection

began when a group of Negroes set out for St. Augustine and freedom, killing all whites they met on the way. They were quickly surrounded and the entire group was massacred. The death toll is 21 whites and 44 Negroes. A similar revolt occurred near the Stono River when a slave named Cato led a large group of Negroes against whites. Before the Stono Rebellion could be put down, 30 whites and a larger number of Negroes were dead. Yet another revolt took place in Berkeley County at St. John's Parish . . ."

In 1741, an article from a newspaper in New York City entitled, <u>Suspected of arson, 29 slaves executed</u>, revealed the following:
"A series of suspicious fires has occurred across New York city this year, and many people have linked the arson to Negroes slaves, who, it is alleged, were aiming to take control of the city. As a result, 11 Negroes have been burned at the stake and 18 hanged. Four poor whites were also implicated in the crimes and hanged."

A colonial newspaper of July 7, 1759 explained:

THE RACIALIZATION OF SLAVERY

"The Ship 'Polly,' Capt. Hamilton, and the Ship 'Mercury,' Capt. Ingledieu both of Bristol, were lately lost on the Coast of Africa. Capt. Hamilton was destined for this Port with a Cargo of Slaves. A Sloop commanded by a brother of the above Capt. Ingledieu, slaving up the River Gambia, was attacked by a Number of the Natives, about the 27th of February last, and made a good defence; but the Captain finding himself desperately wounded, and likely to be overcome, rather than fall into the Hands of such merciless Wretches, when about 80 Negroes had boarded his Vessel, discharged a Pistol into his Magazine, and blew her up; himself and every Soul on Board perished. The Snow 'Perfect,' Capt. William Potter, of Liverpool, bound for this Port, is also cut off by the Negroes in the River Gambia and every Man on board murdered; and the Vessel lost. According to some Accounts that have been received, there is Reason to fear, that the Ship 'Pearl,' of and from Bristol, Henry Todd, Master, bound for Gambia and this Port, was lost in coming out."

AFRICAN FREEDOM FIGHTERS

This newsletter from Annapolis Maryland in August 1759 states:
"Friday evening last arrived here in about six weeks from Gambia, the Ship Upton, Capt. Thomas Birch, with upwards of 200 very likely, healthy slaves, which are allowed by Judges to be as choice a parcel of Negroes as has ever been imported into this Province. Capt Birch on his outward bound Passage, took a French letter of Marque Ship with 8 Carriage and 12 Swivel Guns and 50 Men, after a very smart engagement of two hours and a half, one glass of which time they were so close as to be lock'd together: In the engagement the French Captain and 12 of his men were killed, and 16 wounded. Capt. Birch had but 30 odd men, one which was killed, and 5 or 6 wounded . . ."

An Albany New York newspaper printed this article in 1793, Slaves burn Albany:
"The fears of some have turned to reality as Negro slaves in Albany set fires that caused damage totaling a quarter of a million dollars. Three men and two women are now being held, awaiting execution for the crime of arson. Fear of

THE RACIALIZATION OF SLAVERY

Negro uprisings has been fairly widespread recently. In August, the Virginia cities of Richmond, Powhatan and Elizabeth City sent requests to their Governor for arms to quell rumored and actual rebellions."

In 1802 another paper would write, <u>Slave uprisings plague South; slavery curbed in Northern states</u>:
"In North Carolina, at least six counties have reported slave conspiracies recently, including a plot in May led by the outlaw Tom Cooper . . . Virginia has also been the scene of many insurrections. Alleged conspiracies in Richmond, Williamburg, Brunswick, Norfolk, Princess Anne, Hanover County, Halifax and elsewhere have resulted in the banishing, flogging or hanging of a large number of slaves. Some white men, as well as Negroes, were reported to be involved in the revolutionary plot in Halifax . . ."

Here is an 1811 article from a New Orleans paper, <u>Slaves killed in rebellion; heads shown</u>:

AFRICAN FREEDOM FIGHTERS

"A rebellion of more than 400 slaves that began two days ago has forced many white residents of the parishes of St. Charles and St. John the Baptist to flee to safety in New Orleans. The rebellion began at the plantation of Major Andry when slaves armed with cane knives, axes, clubs and a few guns killed Andry's son and marched on to other plantations, destroying them and killing at least one other white. The rebellion was led by Charles Deslondes, a free mulatto from Haiti; and other rebels were said to be local slaves. Yesterday, the insurrection was opposed by a group of planters led by Major Andry, who pursued the slaves and caught and executed many. Today, the militia and state troops were called out, surrounding the remaining rebels. In all, 66 slaves were killed; their heads were strung up along the road from New Orleans to Andry's plantation. In another incident involving slaves, white forces were sent to annihilate a fugitive slave community in Cabbarrus County, North Carolina. At least two slaves were killed and the others were captured."

The Racialization of Slavery

One of the Connecticut newspapers put this story out in 1839, <u>Africans held after slave revolt at sea:</u>

"A battered Spanish slave ship has arrived off the coast of Connecticut with 53 Africans in command. According to the two surviving crew members, the Amistad was headed from one Cuban port to another when the slaves on board rebelled. Led by a Mendi tribesmen named Cinque, they killed the captain and nearly all the crew, leaving only two alive to sail north. Spain is expected to demand extradition of the rebels."

In 1851, a Boston newspaper reported, <u>Negroes storm jail, free fugitive slave:</u>

"An angry mob of free Negroes stormed a jail here today and released a slave named Shadrach, who had been arrested under the new federal Fugitive Slave Law, valid even in free states. To claim a runaway, a master need only show an affidavit proving ownership. Bounties are often paid for runaways."

Finally here, on many occasions Frederick Douglass paid homage to individuals who made heroic sacrifices in the cause of freedom. Here is one such tribute:

"Hence, my friends, every mother who, like Margaret Garner, plunges a knife into the bosom of her infant to save it from the hell of Christian Slavery, should be held and honored as a benefactress. Every fugitive from slavery who like the noble William Thomas at Wilkesbarre, prefers to perish in a river made red by his own blood, to submission to the hell hounds who were hunting and shooting at him, should be esteemed as a glorious martyr, worthy to be held in grateful memory by our people. The fugitive Horace, at Mechanicsburgh, Ohio, the other day, who taught the slave catchers from Kentucky that it was safer to arrest white men than to arrest him, did a most excellent service to our cause. Parker and his noble band of fifteen at Christiana, who defended themselves from the kidnappers with prayers and pistols, are entitled to the honor of making the first successful resistance to the Fugitive Slave Bill. But for that resistance, and the rescue of Jerry, and Shadrack, the man-hunters would have hunted our hills and valleys

THE RACIALIZATION OF SLAVERY

here with the same freedom with which they now hunt their own dismal swamps. There was an important lesson in the conduct of that noble Krooman in New York, the other day, who, supposing that the American Christians were about to enslave him, betook himself to the mast head, and with knife in hand, said he would cut his throat before he would be made a slave. Joseph Cinque on the deck of the Amistad, did that which should make his name dear to us. He bore nature's burning protest against slavery. Madison Washington who struck down his oppressor on the deck of the Creole, is more worthy to be remembered than the colored man who shot Pitcairn at Bunter Hill..."[5]

---

[5] Donnan, E., Documents Illustrative of the History of the Slave Trade to America Vol. II, p. 1, Vol. IV, pp. 34 - 35, 374 & Halasz, N., The Rattling Chains p. 9 & Chronicle of America p. 101, 102, 211, 228, 246, 311, 340 & International Library of Negro Life and History: Historical Negro Biographies pp. 63 - 64 & Aptheker, H., American Negro Slave Revolts pp. 155, 163 - 165 & Hornsby, A., Chronology of African American History p. 3 & Rosen, R., A Short History of Carolina pp. 70 - 73 & Foner, P., Life and Writings of Frederick Douglass Vol. II, pp. 437 - 438
Incidentally, the first recorded slave revolt in the British Colonies in North America took place in 1663. Hornsby says,

One quick point: I would be remiss not to explain that conflicts and causality figures in American papers were only presented in a way that was amenable to slavers.[6] Furthermore, reports of successful rebellions and escapes were covered up. In deference here to Aptheker:

> *"It was the practice of the rulers of the South to censor news of slave unrest. Specific admissions and evidences of this are numerous."*

Consequently, <u>many great acts of individual courage and heroism were not reported, even when plainly known, by the American press</u>.

The truth is that many Caucasians and Africans were to loose their lives in bloody insurrections from New York to Louisiana. American

---

"The first major conspiracy of people in servitude was documented in Colonial America. A plot of white servants and black slaves was betrayed by a servant in Glouster County, Virginia."

[6] Kick, R., <u>You Are Being Lied To</u>
Selective media reporting continues to this day . . .

THE RACIALIZATION OF SLAVERY

historians actually placing the number in which ten or more Africans took up arms against slavers at 250.[7]

---

[7] Aptheker, H., <u>American Negro Slave Revolts</u> pp. 140 - 141, 162 & James, C., <u>A History of Negro Revolt</u> & Hornsby, A., <u>Chronology of African American History</u> & Hornsby, A., <u>The Black Almanac</u> & <u>International Library of Negro Life and History: Historical Negro Biographies</u> & <u>Chronicle of America</u>

Upon occasion Africans would gain their freedom by other than violent means. Aptheker remarks, *"In considering the subject of slave insurrections it is proper to bear in mind that it forms but one method used by the Negroes in fighting against enslavement. There were several others which must be considered. As has already been observed, it was often possible for the slave, by great perseverance and labor, to purchase his own freedom and, this being accomplished, the freedom of those dear to him. It is not possible to say how many Negroes were thus emancipated, but it is probable that thousands actually ransomed themselves or those they loved. Another method by which an indeterminate number, but again probably thousands, gained their freedom was by serving in the Army and Navy of the Republic during the War for Independence. Flight was a major factor in the battle against bondage. Slaves fled wherever havens of liberation appeared, to the Spaniards, Mexicans, Dutch, Canadians, French; to the armies of Britain and France; and, of course, to the army of Lincoln; to mountains, forests, and swamps in the South (often establishing camps therein); and, along the routes of the Underground Railroad. The figures here again must be only guesses, but it is probable that hundreds of thousands in the course of slavery succeeded in gaining liberty by flight. Estimates for the Underground Railroad alone have been summarized by W. B. Hesseltine as follows:*

African Freedom Fighters

Sojourner Truth c. 1864

'Between 1830 and 1860 as many as 2,000 slaves a year passed into the land of the free along the routes of the Underground Railroad.'"

THE RACIALIZATION OF SLAVERY

Harriet Tubman c. 1865

Some of the most celebrated Black freedom fighters were Frederick Douglass, Harriet

Tubman, Sojourner Truth, Gabriel Prosser, Nat Turner, Charles Lennox Redmond, James McCrummel, Robert Purvis, Henry Highland Garnet, Samuel Ward, James Barbadoes, Samuel Cornish, Lewis Sheridan Leary, Denmark Vessey, Theodore Wright, Peter Williams, Gideon Jackson, Mammy Pleasants and James Forten.[8]

---

[8] Quarles, B., Black Abolitionists & The International Library of Negro Life and History: Historical Negro Biographies & Milele, N., The Journey of the Songhai People pp. 125 - 142 & Wesley, C., The International Library of Negro Life and History: Negro Americans And the Civil War & Gladstone, W., United States Colored Troops & Chronicle of America pp. 102, 211, 215, 263, 316, 318, 340, 350, 362 & Halasz, N., The Rattling Chains & Rosen, R., A Short History of Carolina pp. 70 - 73 & Rogers, J.A., Sex and Race Vol. III, pp. 309 - 315 & Katz, W., Black Indians: A Hidden Heritage
It should be noted as well that the Seminoles (a union of Native Americans and Africans who had escaped the slavers) would conduct a staunch resistance to the United States for many years. A Florida news article of 1842 reported: *"The so-called Second Seminole War has finally ended. This struggle, which pitted the United States Army against the Seminole Indians and their runaway Negro slave allies under Chief Osceola, began five years ago when the Indians refused to be moved west of the Mississippi River. Rejecting Andrew Jackson's Indian removal policy, they launched a vicious war that cost the American government over $20 million. Of the 10,000 soldiers who fought in this conflict, 1500 died in*

The Racialization of Slavery

While this has been brief, it clearly illustrates the fact that despite being outnumbered, outgunned, and an ocean away from their homeland—many Africans were to fight valiantly for their freedom, and the liberty of others . . .

White Abolitionists

To conclude this discussion without acknowledging the fact that many Whites were to philosophically, financially and martially oppose slavery before the Civil War—would be contemptible in my veiw. Inasmuch as they have widely been deemed the fairest and most morally ethical of the settlers—it comes as no surprise that many Quakers (their most

---

action. Despite victory, such losses are probably both bitter and ironic for the former President, who once boasted that with 50 women, he 'could whip every Indian that had ever crossed the Suwannee.'"

celebrated leader being William Penn) should represent a substantial number of the ranks of the early abolitionists. The Quakers' formal opposition to slavery began in 1688.

The mantle of the abolitionist movement's most eloquent and prolific White spokesman, fell to the Boston writer William Lloyd Garrison. Yet, for so much as no one would critique the blight of slavery better—let me share an excerpt from the writings of the Southern abolitionist, Hinton C. Helper:

> *"It is amusing to ignorance, amazing to credulity, and insulting to intelligence, to hear them in their blathering efforts to mystify and pervert the sacred principles of liberty, and turn the curse of slavery into a blessing. To the illiterate poor whites—made poor and ignorant by the system of slavery—they hold out the idea that slavery is the very bulwark of our*

liberties, and the foundation of American independence . . . We want to become an auxiliary in the good work, and facilitate it. The liberation of five millions of 'poor white trash' from the second degree of slavery, and of three millions of miserable kidnapped negroes from the first degree . . . It now behooves us to take a bold and determined stand in defence of the inalienable rights of ourselves and of our fellow men, and to avenge the multiplicity of wrongs, social and political, which we have suffered at the hands of a villainous oligarchy. It is madness to delay."[9]

---

[9] Lacy, D., The Abolitionists & Helper, H., The Impending Crisis of the South pp. 25 - 33, 42 - 43, 53, 80 - 82, 87, 92 - 93, 406 - 407 & The Suppressed Book About Slavery pp. 233 - 234 & Tuttle, F., & Perry, J., An Economic History of the United States p. 154 & Chronicle of America pp. 352 - 354, 407 & Montagu, A., Man's Most Dangerous Myth: The Fallacy of Race pp. 228 - 231 & Benedict, R., & Weltfish, G., The Races of Mankind pp. 17 - 18 & Worthy, R., The Founders' Façade: Christianity, Democracy, Freemasonry, and the founding of America pp. 27 - 38

AFRICAN FREEDOM FIGHTERS

Additionally, *and make no mistake about this,* White abolitionists did a great deal more than pay lip service. For instance, Art Tappan and

---

Helper's evaluation had clear merit as of the South's 5 million Whites—less than 2,000 (0.04%) owned large plantations. Chroniclers make the following assessment of life in the South during slavery: *"Nor is the non-Slaveholding white portion of the population scarcely in a better condition. Ignorance is an 'Institution' in the Slaveholding States. It is a political necessity, and is as much provided for by legislation and by 'public sentiment,' and guarded by enactments, as intelligence is in the 'free states.' It must be. The restrictions, which keep it from the Slaves keep from the 'free whites,' excepting, always, the few who live at the top."* It is also noteworthy that despite the South's portrayal as an agricultural treasure chest, profits from the agricultural harvests of the free Northern states would eventually leave the slave states behind. Helper explained that by 1850, the height of slavery, the North's agricultural output far exceeded that in the South. The South's principal crops were cotton, tobacco, rice, hemp and sugar cane. Yet, crop yields of the North's hay crop alone were more profitable than all of these Southern crops put together. But nothing illustrates Helper's pronouncement more clearly than the fact that despite racism and the generational impediments to education that Blacks faced in the North—IQ tests administered by the United States Army in 1943 revealed that Black recruits from Northern states had higher IQs than White recruits from the South. To quote Montagu, *"The tests showed that Negroes from certain Northern states on the whole did better in the tests than white recruits from almost all the Southern states."* What clearer illustration could there be of the effect of allowing one's self to be duped by despots?

The Racialization of Slavery

Gerrit Smith were two of the movement's largest financial bakers. On the literary front, Harriet Beecher Stowe would probably do as much as anyone to bring the ills of slavery into the homes of White Northerners with her, <u>Uncle Tom's Cabin</u>. In truth, millions of White men and women would play some part in bringing down slavery; but perhaps, the bravest and most committed of them all was John Brown.

John Brown c. 1856

While many would encourage boycotts, civil disobedience, stress education for Blacks, harbor runaways, register Blacks to vote, and even publicly burn copies of the Constitution—Brown would actually take up arms for this cause. Financed by former slave Mammy Pleasants, the militant Brown, (*who often drew parallels between Africans in America and the Jews of ancient Egypt*) was so dedicated to the abolition of slavery that on October 16, 1859, he and twenty of his followers captured the nation's arsenal at Harpers Ferry!

Although Brown was successful in taking the arsenal, his plan was thwarted because his hope to quickly arm the slaves of the area and overthrow the slaveholders never took shape. Consequently, shortly after the take over, General Lee and his militia surrounded and subdued Brown's forces. Tried for his many battles with the slavers, and his raid on Harpers

The Racialization of Slavery

Ferry—Brown was found guilty and sentenced to death. At one with his convictions to the end, after hearing the court's verdict John would boldly declare:

> *"I am yet too young to understand that God is any respect of persons, I believe that to have interfered as I have done—as I have freely admitted I have done—in behalf of His despised poor, was not wrong, but right! Now, if it is deemed necessary that I should forfeit my life for the furtherance of the ends of justice, and mingle my blood further with the blood of my children and with the blood of millions in this slave country whose rights are disregarded by wicked, cruel, and unjust enactments, I say, let it be done!"*[10]

---

[10] Quarles, B., Black Mosaic pp. 67 - 79 & Lacy, D., The Abolitionists pp. 102 - 103 & Duignan, P., & Clendenen, C., The United States and the African Slave Trade 1619 - 1862 p. 14 & Halasz, N., The Rattling Chains pp. 198 - 199, 231 - 237 & The Writings of Henry D. Thoreau (net) & Chronicle of America p. 128

Regardless as to race, all of the abolitionists mentioned here were truly extraordinary souls: by petitioning the Congress to abolish slavery; by creating anti-slavery newspapers; by raising funds; by even running and electing candidates to the Congress—White abolitionists would strike many effective blows against the institution of racial slavery in America.

A few of the most widely celebrated abolitionists were William Lloyd Garrison, John Brown, Benjamin Lundy, Charles Grandison Finney, Lucretia Mott, Elizabeth Cady Stanton, John Greenleaf Whittier, Art and Lewis Tappan, Lucy B. Stone, Lydia Maria Child, James G. Birney, Theodore Weld, Sarah and Angelina Grimke, Harriet Beecher Stowe, Gerrit Smith, John Hale, Ralph Waldo Emerson, Maria Weston Chapman,

---

The Quakers were also at the forefront of the cause of women's rights in America. At the Quakers annual meeting in 1767, 25 of their 60 leaders were women. Photo of John Brown (page 204) appears courtesy of U.S. Dept. of Defense.

Thaddeus Stevens, David R. Wilmont, Amos Dresser, Elijah P. Lovejoy and Henry David Thoreau.[11]

William Lloyd Garrison c. 1870

---

[11] Ibid.,
Photo appears courtesy of The National Archives and Records Admin.

As we close, allow me to simply say that the quintessential understanding driving all of these individuals, Black and White, is probably best synthesized and expressed here by the heralded Frederick Douglass:

> "Let me give you a word of the philosophy of reform. The whole history of the progress of human liberty shows that all concessions yet made to her august claims, have been born of earnest struggle. The conflict has been exciting, agitating, all-absorbing, and for the time being, putting all other tumults to silence. It must do this or it does nothing. If there is no struggle there is no progress. Those who profess to favor freedom and yet depreciate agitation, are men who want crops without plowing up the ground, they want rain without thunder and lightning. They want the ocean without the awful roar of its many waters. This struggle may be a

The Racialization of Slavery

moral one, or it may be a physical one, and it may be both moral and physical, but it must be a struggle. Power concedes nothing without a demand. It never did and it never will. Find out just what any people will quietly submit to and you have found out the exact measure of injustice and wrong which will be imposed on them, and these will continue till they are resisted with either words or blows, or with both. The limits of tyrants are prescribed by the endurance of those whom they oppress. In light of these ideas, Negroes will be hunted at the North, and held and flogged at the South so long as they submit to those devilish outrages, and make no resistance, either moral or physical. Men may not get all they pay for in this world, but they must certainly pay for all they get. If we ever get free from the oppressions and wrongs heaped upon us, we must pay for their removal. We must do this by labor, by suffering, by sacrifice, and if needs be, by our lives and the lives of others . . ."[12]

Frederick Douglas c. 1880

---

[12] Foner, P., The Life and Writings of Frederick Douglass Vol. II, pp. 104, 437 - 438 & Seldes, G., The Great Quotations p. 748

The phrase *"Power concedes nothing without a demand"* appears to have first been penned by Douglass in a letter to Gerrit Smith in 1849. He later delivered it in 1857, in a speech at Canandaigua in celebration of the emancipation of the British West Indies. Photo appears courtesy of Dept. of Rare Books & Special Collections – Univ. of Rochester Lib.

Epilogue

EPILOGUE

This is for the mature

For so much as race has been a tremendous hindrance to human progress in these past few centuries—I hope that you will reflect upon the information in this book. You see, regardless of color, until you appreciate the fact that slavery was only recently racialized—you will not reach your optimal potential. This is not merely because you've consigned yourself to moral dwarfdom—but surrendered to those whose "<u>stated design</u>" is to render you steak on a platter . . .

Bibliography

BIBLIOGRAPHY

Aime, S., Fasano, M., Terreno, E., & Groombridge, C., <u>NMR studies of melanins: characterization of a soluble melanin free acid from Sepia ink</u> Pigment Cell Research Vol. 4, No. 5 - 6 Dec. 1991 pp. 216 - 221

Akbar, N., Chains and Images of Psychological Slavery New Mind Productions 1984

Altman, S., The Encyclopedia of African-American Heritage Facts on File 1997

Anderson, A., Scottish Annals from English Chroniclers: AD 500 - 1286 D.N. Nutt 1908

Aoumiel, Dancing Shadows: The Roots of Western Religious Beliefs Llewellyn 1994

Aptheker, H., American Negro Slave Revolts International Publ. 1943

Augarde, T., The Oxford Dictionary of Modern Quotations Oxford 1991

Baker, H., The Colored Inventor Arno Press 1969

Baltazar, E., The Dark Center Paulist Press 1973

Bauval, R., & Gilbert, A., The Orion Mystery Crown Pub. 1994

Beard, J., The Life of Toussaint L'Ouverture Greenwood 1975

Becker, U., The Continuum Encyclopedia of Symbols Continuum Acad. 2005

Benedict, R., Race: Science and Politics Viking Press 1943

Benedict, R., & Weltfish, G., The Races of Mankind Columbia Univ. 1943

Berlitz, C., Atlantis: The Eighth Continent Putnam & Sons 1984

Bernal, I., The Olmec World Univ. of Berkley Press 1969

Biedermann, H., Dictionary of Symbolism Facts on File 1992

Birley, A., Septimius Severus: The African Emperor Doubleday 1972

Bishop, M., The Horizon Book of the Middle Ages American Heritage American Heritage & Bonanza Books 1968

Blake, W., History of Slavery and the Slave Trade Miller 1858

Boorstin, D., The Discoverers Random House 1985

Brackman, H., The Ebb and Flow of Conflict: A History of Black Jewish Relations through 1900 (Ph.D. diss., UCLA 1977)

Bradley, M., The Black Discovery of America Personal Library 1981

Briggs, A., A Social History of England Viking Press 1983

Brodie, F., Thomas Jefferson: An Intimate History Norton 1974

BIBLIOGRAPHY

Brodie, J., Created Equal: the lives and ideas of Black American innovators Morrow 1993

Brooks, L., Great Civilizations of Ancient Africa Four Winds Press 1963

Brown, T., Black Lies, White Lies William Morrow & Co. 1995

Budge, E.A., A History of Egypt Anthropological Pub. 1968

Budge, E.A., A History of Ethiopia Anthropological Pub. 1966

Budge, E.A., A Short History of the Egyptian People Dent 1923

Budge, E.A., Amulets and Talismans Citadel Press 1992

Budge, E.A., Osiris: & The Egyptian Religion of Resurrection Vol. I - II Univ. Books 1961

Budge, E.A., The Book of the Dead Arkana 1985

Burn, A., & Selincourt, A., Herodotus the Histories Penguin 1972

Butler, S., Speech on Interventionism http://www.the7thfire.com/Politics%20and%20History/Gen-Smedley-Butler.htm 1-19-9

Butzer, C. (ed.), Ancient Egypt: Discovering Its Splendors National Geographic Soc. 1978

Bylinsky, G., Mass Producing Nature's Sun Screen Fortune Vol. 125, No. 11 Jun. 1, 1992 p. 131

Campbell, M., The Maroons Africa World Press 1990

Chadwick, C., Potten, C., Cohen, A., & Young, A., The time of onset and duration of 5-methoxypsoralen photochemoprotection from UVR-induced DNA damage in human skin British Journal of Dermatology Vol. 131, No. 4 Oct. 1994 pp. 483 - 494

Chang, K., Jefferson Fathered Slave Son http://www.abcnews.com/sections/science/DailyNews/jefferson981031.html 11-7-98

Chedekel, M., Murr, B., & Zeise, L., Melanin standard method: empirical formula Pigment Cell Research Vol. 5, No. 3 Sept. 1992 pp. 143 - 147

Clegg, R., Mackey's Revised History of Freemasonry The Masonic History Co. 1898

Collins, R., Medes and Persians: Conquers & Diplomats McGraw-Hill 1972

Connah, G., African Civilization Cambridge Univ. Press 1987

Coon, C., Racial Adaptations Nelson – Hall 1982

Cox, G., African Empires and Civilizations African Heritage Studies Publ. 1974

Curtin, P., The Atlantic Slave Trade: A Census Univ. of Wis. 1969

David, R., The Egyptian Kingdoms Elsevier & Phaidon 1975

Davidoff, H., The Pocket Book of Quotations Pocket 1942

BIBLIOGRAPHY

Davidson, B., Africa in History Macmillan 1974

Davidson, B., History of West Africa to the Nineteenth Century Anchor Books 1966

Davidson, B., The Lost Cities of Africa Little, Brown and Co. 1970

Davis, C., Western Awakening Appleton, Century, Crofts 1967

Davis, E., The First Sex Putnam & Sons 1971

De Graft-Johnson, J., African Glory Black Classic Press 1954

De Lubicz, R., Sacred Science: The King of Pharaonic Theocracy Inner Traditions International 1961

Diffey, B., Healy, E., Thody, A., & Rees, J., Melanin, melanocytes, and melanoma Lancet Vol. 346, No. 8991 - 8992 Dec. 23, 1995 p. 1713

Diggs, E., Black Chronology Hall 1983

Diggs, I., Black Innovators Inst. of Positive Ed. 1975

Diop, C.A., Civilization or Barbarism Lawrence Hill Books 1981

Diop, C.A., The African Origin of Civilization: Myth Or Reality Lawrence Hill Books 1974

Donnan, E., Documents Illustrative of the History of the Slave Trade to America Vol. I - IV Carnegie Institute 1930 - 1935

Drozdz, R., Siegrist, W., Baker, B., Chluba de Tapia, J., & Eberle, A., Melanin-concentrating hormone binding to mouse melanoma cells in vitro Febs Letters Vol. 359, No. 2 - 3 Feb. 13, 1995 pp. 199 - 202

Dubois, F., Timbuctoo the Mysterious W. Heinemann, 1897

Duckat, W., Beggar to King Doubleday 1968

Duignan, P., & Clendenen, C., The United States and the African Slave Trade 1619 - 1862 Greenwood Press 1978

Elkins, S., Slavery Univ. of Chicago 1976

Faber, E., Jews, Slaves, and the Slave Trade NYU Press 1998

Fischman, J., Putting Our Oldest Ancestors in their Proper Places Science Vol. 265, No. 5181 Sept. 30, 1994 pp. 2011 - 2013

Fogel, R., Time on the Cross Little, Brown & Co. 1974

Foner, P., The Life and Writings of Frederick Douglass Vol. II International Publ. 1950

Forbes, J., Black Africans and Native Americans Blackwell 1988

Franch, J., & Paris, I., (tr.), Pre-Columbian Art Abrams 1983

Gaskell, G., Dictionary of all Scriptures and Myths Julien Press 1960

BIBLIOGRAPHY

Gladstone, W., United States Colored Troops Thomas Publ. 1990

Gordon, C., Before Columbus Crown Publ. 1971

Gore, A., Earth in the Balance Penguin 1992

Gouldner, A., The Hellenic World Basic Books 1965

Grant, M., The Roman Emperors Scribner & Sons 1985

Grogan, D., & Harrison, L., <u>Finding the Link</u> People Weekly Vol. 42, No. 24 Dec. 12, 1994 pp. 165 – 167

Gunn, B., The Instruction of Ptahhotep and the Instruction of Kegemni: The Oldest Books in the World

Haber, L., Black Pioneers of Science and Invention Harcourt, Brace & World 1970

Halasz, N., The Rattling Chains McKay Co. 1966

Haley, A., Roots Dell 1974

Hall, M., The Secret Teachings of All Ages The Philosophical Research Soc. 1977

Hallett, R., Africa Since 1875 Univ. of Mich. 1974

Harvey, L. Islamic Spain: 1250 to 1500 U. of Chicago 1990

Haynes, R., Blacks in White America Before 1865 McKay Co. 1972

Helper, H., The Impending Crisis of the South Burdick Bros. 1857

Herm, G., Phoenicians Morrow 1975

Heurgon, J., Daily Life of the Etruscans Macmillan 1964

Higgins, G., Anacalypsis University Books 1965

Hoebel, E., Anthropology: The Study of Man McGraw-Hill 1956

Hoffer, P., Law and People in Colonial America John Hopkins 1992

Hornsby, A., Chronology of African American History Gale 1991

Hornsby, A., The Black Almanac Barren's Educational Inc. 1972

Howarth, D., 1066: The Year of the Conquest Penguin 1977

Hoyt, R., Life and Thought in the Middle Ages Lund Press 1967

Huart, C., A History of Arabic Literature Khayats 1966

Hudson, H., The Story of the Renaissance Cassell 1912

Jackson, P., When Roots Die Univ. of Georgia 1987

James, C., A History of Negro Revolt Haskell House 1969

Jeal, T., Livingstone Jeal 1973

Jeffery, G., Schutz, G., & Montoliu, L., <u>Correction of abnormal pathways found with albinism by introduction of a functional tyrosinase gene in transgenic mice</u>

BIBLIOGRAPHY

Developmental Biology Vol. 166, No. 2 Dec. 1994 pp. 460 - 464

Jenkins, W., Pro-Slavery thought in the Old South Univ. of North Carolina 1960

Jones, C., Africa: 1500 - 1900 Facts on File 1993

Katz, W., Black Indians: A Hidden Heritage Ethrac 1986

Keating, R., Nubian Twilight Harcourt, Brace & World 1963

Keith, A., The Belgian Congo and the Berlin Act Clarendon 1919

Keller, W., The Etruscans Knopf 1974

Kephart, C., Races of Mankind N.Y. Philosophical Lib. 1960

Kick, R., (ed.), YOU ARE BEING LIED TO: The Disinformation Guide to Media, Historical Whitewashes and Cultural Myths The Disinformation Company LTD 2001

Kimura, N., & Tsuge, T., Gene cluster involved in Melanin biosynthesis of the filamentous fungus Alternaria alternata Journal of Bacteriology Vol. 175, No. 13 - 14 July 1993 pp. 4427 - 4429

King, A., Quotations in Black Greenwood Press 1981

Kittles, R., Nature, origin, and variation of human pigmentation Journal of Black Studies Vol. 26, No. 1 pp. 36 - 58

Klein, H., The Middle Passage Princeton Univ. Press 1978

Koch, R., The Book of Signs Dover 1955

Lacy, D., The Abolitionists McGraw-Hill 1978

Lane-Poole, S., The Moors in Spain T.F. Unwin 1888

Lemonick, M., Everyone's Genealogical Mother: Biologists Speculate "Eve" lived in Sub-Saharan Africa Time Vol. 129, No. 4 Jan. 26, 1987 p. 66

Lewin, R., & Foley, R., Principles of Human Evolution Blackwell 2003

Lillyquist, M., Sunlight & Health: The Positive and Negative Effects of the Sun on You pp. 2, 16, 19 - 21, 59, 67, 77 - 80

Lord, S., Forever Younger Vogue Vol. 182, No. 8 Aug. 1992 p. 242

Lurker, M., The Gods and Symbols of Ancient Egypt Thames & Hudson 1980

Lynch, J., Spain: 1516 - 1598 Blackwell 1991

Madariaga, S., The Four Voyages of Columbus Ungar 1940

Malcioln, J., The African Origins of Modern Judaism Africa World Press 1996

Maltz, M., The Magic Power of Self-Image Psychology Pocket Books 1970

Mannix, D., Black Cargoes Viking Press 1962

McCray, W., The Black Presence in the Bible Black Light Fellowship 1990

BIBLIOGRAPHY

Mencken, H., A New Dictionary of Quotations Knopf 1977

Mercado, J., Garcia, F., Fernandez, M., & Olivares, J., Melanin production by Rizobium melilotti GR4 is linked to nansymbiotic plasmid pRmeGR4b: cloning, sequencing, and expression of the tyrosinase gene mepA Journal of Bacteriology Vol. 175, No. 17 - 18 Sept. 1993 pp. 5403 - 5408

Meyer, M., & Sherman, W., The Course of Mexican History Oxford Univ. Press 1987

Milele, N., The Journey of the Songhai People Pan African Fed. 1987

Montagu, A., Man's Most Dangerous Myth: The Fallacy of Race The World Publ. Co. 1964

Montagu, A., The Concept of Race Free Press 1964

Muller, M., Mythology of All Races Vol. XII Cooper Square 1964

Murphy, E., Diodorus on Egypt McFarland 1985

Notestein, W., The English People on the Eve of Colonization 1603 - 1630 Harper & Row 1954

Oates, J., Babylon Thames & Hudson 1979

Okihiro, G., In Resistance: Studies in African, Caribbean and Afro- American History Univ. of Mass. 1986

Opie, I., & Tatem, M., A Dictionary of Superstitions Oxford Univ. 1989

Owen, F., The Germanic People Bookman Assoc. 1960

Pierpaoli, W., Regelson, W., & Colman, C., The Melantonin Miracle: Nature's Age-Reversing, Disease-Fighting, Sex-Enhancing Hormone Simon & Schuster 1995

Pike, A., Morals and Dogma of the Ancient and Accepted Scottish Rite of Freemasonry Charleston A∴M∴ 5641

Platt, S., Respectfully Quoted Library of Congress 1989

Ploski, H., & Kaiser, E., Negro Almanac Bellwether Co. 1971

Puckett, N., Black Names in America: Origins and Usage G.K. Hall 1975

Quarles, B., Black Abolitionists Oxford Press 1969

Quarles, B., Black Mosaic Univ. of Mass 1988

Rawley, J., The Transatlantic Slave Trade: A History Norton 1981

Reeves, N., Into the Mummy's Tomb Madison Press 1992

Richardson, H., & Sayles, G., The Governance of Mediaeval England Edinburgh Univ. Press 1963

Robinson, C., Conversion of Europe Longman, Green & Co. 1917

Rogers, J.A., Sex and Race Rogers Publ. 1967

Rogers, J.A., The Five Negro Presidents of the U.S.A. Rogers Publ. 1965

BIBLIOGRAPHY

Rogers, J.A., World's Great Men of Color Macmillan 1972

Rosen, R., A Short History of Charleston Lexikos 1982

Ross, R., The Elite Serial Killers of Lincoln, JFK, RFK & MLK RIE 2001

Rout, L., The African Experience in Spanish America Cambridge Univ. Press 1976

Rowntree, J., The Imperial Drug Trade Methuen & Co. 1905

Saggs, H., Civilization Before Greece and Rome Yale Univ. 1989

Schraermeyer, U., <u>Fine structure of melanogenesis in the ink sac of Sepia officinalis</u> Pigment Cell Research Vol. 7, No. 1 Feb. 1994 pp. 52 – 60

Scullard, H., Roman Britain Thames & Hudson 1979

Sek-kem, G., Melanin and the Next Millennium: The Kem-Wer Factor (Notes of 2nd Annual Kem-Wer Conference 1987) Sek-Kem 1988

Seldes, G., The Great Quotations Pocket Books 1960, 1967

Shapiro, H., Race Mixture Unesco 1953

Simon, L., Iberia and the Mediterranean World of the Middle Ages Brill 1995

Simons, G., Barbarian Europe Timelife 1968

Sjoo, M., & Mor, B., The Great Cosmic Mother Harper & Row 1817

Sloan, I., The Blacks in America 1492 - 1977   Oceana Press 1977

Snowden, F., Blacks in Antiquity   Harvard Univ. Press 1970

Snyder, L., Race: A History of Modern Ethnic Theories   Longmans, Green & Co. 1939

Soames, J., The Coast of Barbary   London 1938

Stewart, W., & Peterson, H., Builders of Latin America   Harper & Bros. 1942

Stuckey, S., Slave Culture   Oxford Press 1987

Sunderland, E., Elements of Human and Social Geography   Sunderland 1973

Sykes, E., Everyman's Dictionary of Non-classical Mythology   Dutton & Sons 1952

Tarn, W., Hellenistic Civilization   Clowes & Sons 1927

Thomas, H., The Slave Trade   Simon & Schuster 1997

Toppin, E., Biographical History of Blacks in America Since 1528   Mc Kay 1971

Tuttle, F., & Perry, J., An Economic History of the United States   Southwestern Publ. 1970

Valverde, P., Healy, E., Jackson, I., Rees, J., & Thody, A., <u>Variants of the melanocyte-stimulating hormone receptor gene are associated with red hair and hair skin in humans</u>   Nature Genetics Vol. 11, No. 3 Nov. 1995 pp. 328 - 330

BIBLIOGRAPHY

Van Sertima, I., Blacks in Science: Ancient and Modern Transactions 1983

Van Sertima, I., Golden Age of the Moor Transaction Pub. 1993

Van Sertima, I., They Came Before Columbus Random House 1977

Waddell, W., Manetho, Ptolemy Harvard Univ. Press 1948

Ward, P., A Dictionary of Common Fallacies Prometheus Books 1989

Warmington, B., Carthage Penguin 1964

Warmington, B., The North African Provinces Greenwood Press 1971

Warren, R., The Nile McGraw Hill 1968

Wasserstein, A., Flavius Josephus Viking Press 1974

Waszink, J., De Anima Meulenhoff 1947

Watson, A., The Law of the Ancient Romans S.M.U. Press 1970

Watson, P., Egyptian Pyramids and Mastaba Tombs Shire Publ. 1987

Watson, T., <u>Revising Human Origins</u> U.S. World and News Report Vol. 117, No. 13 Oct. 3, 1994 p. 67

Watt, W., The Influence of Islam on Medieval Europe Univ. Press 1972

Wesley, C. (ed.), International Library of Negro Life and History Publishing Co. 1967

Whiston, W., The Life and Works of Flavius Josephus Holt, Rinehart & Winston 1957

Williams, C., The Destruction of Black Civilization: Great Issues of a Race from 4500 B.C. to 2000 A.D. Third World Press 1974

Wills, C., <u>The Skin We're In</u> Discover Nov. 15, No. 11 Nov. 1994 pp. 79 – 80

Wilson, A., The Developmental Psychology of The Black Child Africana Research Publ. 1978

Wilson, J., Culture of Ancient Egypt Phoenix Books 1951

Windsor, R., From Babylon to Timbuktu Exposition Press 1969

Wood, M., Doomsday: A Search for the Roots of England Facts on File - BBC 1986

Worthy, R., About Black Hair KornerStone Books 2006

Worthy, R., The Founders' Façade: Christianity, Democracy, Freemasonry, and the founding of America KornerStone Books 2004

Worthy, R., YHSVH KornerStone Books 2008

Zeise, L., Murr, B., & Chedekel, M., <u>Melanin standard method: particle description</u> Pigment Cell Research Vol. 5, No. 3 Sept. 1992 pp. 132 - 142

BIBLIOGRAPHY

_____., <u>A new ray of hope on melanoma</u> Patient Care Vol. 30, No. 11 June 15, 1996 p. 14

_____., A Paleo Perspective . . . on Global Warming http://www.ngdc.noaa.gov/paleo/globalwarming/home.htm l 6-29-99

_____., Booknotes: Interview with Robert Skidelsky: John Maynard Keynes Vol. III C-Span 4/02

_____., Cancer Facts and Figures 1998 Amer. Cancer Soc. 1999

_____., Chronicle: Egypt (Video) Arts & Entertainment 1990

_____., Chronicle of America Chronicle Publ. 1989

_____., Collier's Encyclopedia Macmillan 1986 – 1997

_____., Columbia Lippincott Gazetteer Columbia Univ. 1962

_____., Desmond Morris' The Human Animal (Video) BBC/TLC 1999

_____., Dictionary of the Middle Ages Scribner & Sons 1986 –1988

_____., Encyclopaedia Britannica Encyclopaedia Britannica Inc. 1999 – 2002

_____., Encyclopedia Americana Grolier Publ. 2001

_____., Encyclopedia of Human Biology Academic Press 1991

THE RACIALIZATION OF SLAVERY

_____., Encyclopedia of Religion Macmillan 1987

_____., Fairview Health Services: Under Your Skin http://fairview.org/hi/conditions/melanoma.htm 6-13-99

_____., For the People: Interview with Dr. C.A. Diop (Video) L. Middleton 1991

_____., Illustrated Dictionary & Concordance of the Bible Jerusalem Publ. House 1986

_____., Inside the Third Reich: Memoir by Albert Speer Macmillan 1970

_____., Melanoma FAQ http://www.mwt.net/~ctustis/melfaq.html 6-13-99

_____., Merriam Webster's Deluxe Dictionary Merriam-Webster 1998

_____., Merriam Webster's Geographical Dictionary Merriam-Webster 1997

_____., Oprah Winfrey: White Relatives Meet Black Relatives (Video) Harpo Prod. 12-28-95

_____., Priestly Sins: Sex and the Church (Video) H.B.O. 1996

_____., The American Peoples Encyclopedia Spencer Press 1955

_____., The Brain: Our Universe Within (Video) Discovery 1994

_____., The Complete Works of William Shakespeare http://www-tech.mit.edu/shakespeare/ 12-20-98

BIBLIOGRAPHY

_____., The Hour of Our Time: The Legacy of William Cooper (DVD) Ether Films 2006

_____., The Living Body: Skin Deep (Video) Films for the Humanities 1985

_____., The Lost Books of the Bible and the Forgotten Books of Eden Bell 1979

_____., The Mystery of the Sphinx (Video) A Magic Eye North Tower Films Prod. Discovery 1996

_____., The Nature of Things Radar: Images from Space (Video) C.B.C. 1987

_____., The Suppressed Book About Slavery Arno Press 1968

_____., The Western Tradition: The Feudal Order (Video) Annenburg 1989

_____., The Western Tradition: The Middle Ages (Video) Annenburg 1989

_____., The World Book Encyclopedia World Book 1970 – 1999

_____., The Writings of Henry D. Thoreau http://www.library.ucsb.edu/depts/thoreau/bfaq.html 11-29-98

_____., Tony Brown's Journal: A First Hand View of Slavery in Africa (Video) Tony Brown Prod. 1996

_____., Tony Brown's Journal: Tear on the Face of America (Video) Tony Brown Prod. 1986

_____., Writings: Franklin Library of America 1987

Index

Index

A

Aaron	30
Abel	31
Abolitionist	66
199 – 208	
Abraham	167
Achen Glacial Age	3
7	
Al-Jahiz	
(*see Amr ben Bahr*)	
Alabama	85
Albany	189
Albinism	18
22, 44	
Alhambra	54
Amistad	192
Amr ben Bahr	34
35 - 36	
Amulets	118
Andalusia (*see Moors*)	
Andresote, M.	182
Aryan	4
5 - 8, 10	

B

Balboa	73

Barbados	131
132	
Barbot, J.	63
124, 138, 142, 179	
Black Madonna	42
Brandenburgers	129
Brazil	182
British	
West Indies	211
Brown, J.	204
205 - 206	
Butler, S.	95

C

Cain	32
Canada	196
Catholic Church	31
51, 52, 57, 60 – 61, 63 – 67, 71, 74, 93, 98	
Celts (*see Keltic*)	
Charles I	73
74 - 77	
Chinese	113
150	
Chirinos, J.	182
Christ (*see YHSVH*)	
Cleveland	177
Columbus	71
76	
Cortez	73

D

Dance	152
Danes	138
139	
Dark Ages	116
123	
Denmark	149
Dio, C.	105
Dogon	156
Douglass, F.	192
193 – 194, 199, 209 - 211	
Du Bois, W.	132
Dutch	76
126, 129, 137, 141 – 143, 146, 149	

E

Eaton, W.	171
Elamite	8
11, 25	
England	52
55 – 57, 83, 90, 126, 131, 135, 137, 140 – 143, 147, 149, 150, 176, 178, 182	
Etruscans	48

F

Fat/Muscle (*volume*)	13
Fitzhugh	88
89	
Florida	199
France (*see Gaul*)	
Franklin, B.	108
109 - 111	
French (*see Gaul*)	
Freud, S.	117
Fylfot	9
26	

G

Garrison, W.	201
202	
Gaul	48
51, 53, 94, 103, 125 - 126, 129 - 130, 137, 139, 147, 149, 176, 182 – 183, 186 - 187	
Genoese	129
Germany	10
26 - 27, 49 – 51, 53, 94	
Gold Coast	32
59, 61, 128, 137, 142	
Golden Age	123
Greeks	48
49, 103, 120	

INDEX

Guacamaya, M. 182

H

Haley, A. 136, 155
Haiti 182, 191
Ham 38, 39, 42
Hammurabi 166, 167
Harpers Ferry 205
Helper, H. 201, 202 - 203
Higgins, G. iv, vi, 38 – 39, 42, 211, 213
Hispaniola 71, 73, 74
Hitler, A. 10, 27
Hollanders (*see Dutch*)
Human Development 40, 41

I

I.Q. Tests 203

Indentured Servitude 79, 80 - 81
Indus River Valley 4, 11, 16
Interracial Relations 86, 90 – 92

J

Jackson, A. 200
Japheth 38, 39
Jews (*European*) 52, 53, 57, 129, 205
Judas 31

K

Keller, H. 46
Keltic 6, 7, 103
Kung 150

L

Las Casas, B. 74, 75

237

Lincoln, A.	iv, x, 196	Mueller	85, 86 - 88
Livingstone, D.	174	Muhammad	170
Lopes, E.	137, 138		
Louisiana	85, 86, 190 – 191, 196		
L'Ouverture, T.	182, 183		

M

N

Maroons	182	Naaman	31
Maryland	90, 189	Native American	65, 71, 75, 101, 109, 199 – 200
Massachusetts	81, 192	NavioNegreiro	124
Melanin	2, 3, 14, 17 – 25, 43, 165	Nazis	27
Mexico	181	New York	187, 189, 196
Miriam	29, 30	Niger, P.	104
Moors	52, 53 – 55, 57, 59, 63, 97 - 99, 103, 112, 164, 169 - 170	Nile River Valley	16, 155 – 157, 160 - 161
Mortality Rates	133, 134, 135	Noah	38, 39
Moses	29, 30	North Carolina	190, 191
Mourning (*Old World*)	37, 154		

O

Opium Wars	150
Orwell, G.	ix
Osceola	199
Osiris	120, 121

INDEX

P

Palmerston 172
173
Penn, W. 201
Pleasants, M. 205
Portugal (*see subject*)
Prohibitions 57
68, 84 - 85, 90, 98, 101,
149, 170
Ptahhotep iii

Q

Quakers 200
207

R

Rawley, J. 134
Regimento 62
63
Roosevelt, F. 150

S

Sahara Desert 140
153

Saturn 118
Seminoles 199
Severus, S. 104
105
Shakespeare 111
Ship (*slave*) 124
130, 178
Sirius 156
Slave Auction 148
171
Slave Codes 101
170
Slave Store 171
Slavs 39
47, 53, 55
Smith, G. 203
211
Socrates v
South Carolina 65
82, 145, 147, 173, 183, 186
Spain (*see subject*)
Stowe, H. 204
Swastika 9
25 - 27
Swedes 129

T

Tappan, A. 203
Tigris River Valley 11
16

Timeless Wisdom
(see Ptahhotep)

Triangular Trade 131
147, 180

Truth, S. 197
199

Tubman, H. 198
199

Turner, M. 33

Turner, N. 199

U

Uncle Tom's Cabin 204

Underground
Railroad 196
197 - 198

V

Venezuela 182

Victoria 150

Villeins 93

Virginia 84
85, 190, 195

W

Wadstrom, C. 64
176

Weld, T. 172

Wells, H.G. x

Wurm II 3

X

Y

Yahweh
(see YHVH)

Yanga 181
182

YHSVH 42
67, 120

YHVH 29
30

Z

Zipporah 30

Zumbi 182

Past Reviews of the Author's Work!

It is Great!
Jenkins Group Reviewer

Mr. Worthy's research is both—scholarly and important!
**Ms. Pearl Randall, Former Editorial Coordinator
Addison-Wesley**

Beloved R.L. Worthy – Thank you for sharing Truth!
Iyanla Vanzant's Inner Visions Team Member

I love the Book!
Alicia Banks – Radio Talk Show Host

Thank you for the wonderful Book!
Vivian Stringer – Rutgers Women's Basketball Coach

This is a very interesting book!
Megan Sukys – Radio Talk Show Host

A lot has been written on the subject but you're shedding new light!
Barbara Thomas - Northwest African Amer. Museum

Mr. Worthy's ongoing commitment to share much wisdom from experience as another of our vindicationist scholars engage the primary representation of our peoplehood and forge to share our destiny through telling our story—
**Ndugu G.B. T'Ofori-Atta, Professor
Interdenominational Theological Center**

THE RACIALIZATION OF SLAVERY

Discount Order Form

O f course, you can call any of your local bookstores and ask them to order a copy of The Racialization Of Slavery for you for 29.95 plus tax. You should be able to pick your copy up in 48-hours. However, if you would like to have a copy (or copies) delivered to your doorstep and save money—feel free to photocopy this page and use it as an order form. Just fill in the information and mail the <u>discount sale price</u> of $21.95 plus $3.00 shipping and handling for each book to the address below (<u>money orders please</u>). You should receive your order in about a week. For orders of 5 books or more - contact us via email to learn about our volume discounts and <u>online credit card ordering</u> process.

Name:_____

Address:_____

City, State & Zip:_____

Number of Books:_____   Amount Enclosed:_____

{No sales tax outside of Wa. State}

KornerStone Books
6947 Coal Creek Pkwy.
Suite 206
Newcastle, WA. 98059
Ksbooks@execs.com

www.ingramcontent.com/pod-product-compliance
Lightning Source LLC
Chambersburg PA
CBHW070939230426
43666CB00011B/2496